Persian and Caucasus Myths

A Captivating Guide to Persian Mythology and Tales from Circassia, Armenia, and Georgia

© Copyright 2021

The contents of this book may not be reproduced, duplicated, or transmitted without direct written permission from the author.

Under no circumstances will any legal responsibility or blame be held against the publisher for any reparation, damages, or monetary loss due to the information herein, either directly or indirectly.

Legal Notice:

This book is copyright protected. This is only for personal use. You cannot amend, distribute, sell, use, quote, or paraphrase any part of the content within this book without the consent of the author.

Disclaimer Notice:

Please note the information within this document is for educational and entertainment purposes only. Every attempt has been made to provide accurate, up to date, and reliable complete information. No warranties of any kind are expressed or implied. Readers acknowledge that the author is not engaging in the rendering of legal, financial, medical, or professional advice. The content of this book has been derived from various sources. Please consult a licensed professional before attempting any techniques outlined in this book.

By reading this document, the reader agrees that under no circumstances is the author responsible for any losses, direct or indirect, which are incurred because of the use of the information within this document, including, but not limited to, errors, omissions, or inaccuracies.

Free Bonus from Captivating History (Available for a Limited time)

Hi History Lovers!

Now you have a chance to join our exclusive history list so you can get your first history ebook for free as well as discounts and a potential to get more history books for free! Simply visit the link below to join.

Captivatinghistory.com/ebook

Also, make sure to follow us on Facebook, Twitter and Youtube by searching for Captivating History.

Contents

PART 1: PERSIAN MYTHOLOGY 1
    INTRODUCTION 2
    SECTION I: RELIGIOUS MYTHS... 5
    SECTION II: BAKHTIYAR NAMEH 20
    SECTION III: TALES FROM THE SHAHNAMEH 47
PART 2: TALES FROM THE CAUCASUS 91
    INTRODUCTION 92
    SECTION I: MYTHS AND FOLKTALES 96
    SECTION II: NATIONAL EPICS... 116
HERE'S ANOTHER BOOK BY MATT CLAYTON THAT YOU MIGHT LIKE.. 184
FREE BONUS FROM CAPTIVATING HISTORY (AVAILABLE FOR A LIMITED TIME).. 185
BIBLIOGRAPHY.. 186

Part 1: Persian Mythology

Captivating Myths of Gods, Goddesses, Heroes, and Legendary Creatures

Introduction

The Persian Empire was one of the most powerful in the ancient world. Under the Achaemenids, between 500 and 330 BCE, it encompassed a large part of Southwestern Central Asia, including what are now Iran and Afghanistan, and parts of Southern Greece, Eastern Libya and Egypt, the Levant, and part of the Northern Saudi Arabian peninsula. However, at its core was the land that is now Iran, home to some of the world's oldest cultures.

By the third millennium BCE, what was to become Persia became occupied by people who migrated into that area from India. These people called themselves "Aryans," an ancient word in the Avestan language that denotes this particular cultural group and is the root of modern Iran's name.

(Note: The name of this ancient culture has nothing to do with the Third Reich or white supremacist ideology; the word was appropriated for racist uses by Europeans in the nineteenth century.)

The ancient Aryan people kept many of the religious practices and concepts with which they had been familiar in their former home, and these became integrated into the native Persian religion of Zoroastrianism, which was founded c. 1500–1000 BCE by

Zarathustra (aka Zoroaster), a man who purported to have had a vision of Ahura Mazda, the Aryan chief god. Zoroastrianism is essentially dualist, positing Ahura Mazda (Middle Persian "Ohrmazd") as a beneficent creator who vies with Angra Mainyu (Middle Persian "Ahriman"), an evil being whose purpose is to mar and destroy anything made by Ahura Mazda. Zoroastrianism became the official Persian state religion c. 600 BC and is still practiced today, mostly in Iran and India, where it is a minority religion.

Zoroastrian sacred writings are the chief repository of ancient Persian religious myths. Initially, Zoroastrian teachings were transmitted orally; the earliest written texts seem to have been collated during the Sassanian Empire (224-621CE), but the oldest surviving copy is much later, dating from the fourteenth century. The primary collection of these writings is known as the *Avesta* (sometimes called the *Zend-Avesta*), which contains instructions for the performance of religious ceremonies, prayers, moral instruction, sacred laws, and myths concerning Ahura Mazda, Angra Mainyu, and the other sacred cosmic beings who play roles within Zoroastrian religious traditions. The first section of this book is dedicated to Zoroastrian religious tales, both from the *Avesta* and the later *Bundahisn*, another important Zoroastrian sacred document.

Another primary source of ancient Persian myth is the *Shahnameh*, which means "tales of the kings." The *Shahnameh* was compiled between 997 and 1010 CE by Persian poet Abdul Qasem Ferdowsi Tusi (c. 935 or 940-c. 1019 or 1026; often called simply "Ferdowsi"). In its original form, *Shahnameh* is an epic poem that relates the history of the Persian kings, beginning with the earliest mythical rulers and ending with historically accurate tales about the Sasanian Empire. These stories are full of kings' and heroes' exploits, the misdeeds of demons, battles, dragons, and derring-do, making for lively reading. The first few tales in the *Shahnameh* also function as just-so stories, explaining the origins of many human activities and practices, attributed to the wisdom and intelligence of early mythical kings. The tour through Persian myth ends with selections from Ferdowsi's collection of stories, including "The Seven Trials of Rostam," a lengthy tale about the deeds of the most famous and important of all ancient Persian heroes, and his faithful steed, Rakhsh.

In between the sacred stories from the *Avesta* and *Bundahisn* and the secular tales of the *Shahnameh* is an extended excerpt from the *Bakhtiyar Nameh*. The *Bakhtiyar Nameh*, which was compiled in the late sixth or early seventh century CE, consists of a frame story that narrates the life of Bakhtiyar, the title character, in between the sections of which are sandwiched nine folktales told by Bakhtiyar to King Azadbakht. Readers who are familiar with the story of Scheherezade and the tales of the *Arabian Nights* will recognize this structure—since both Scheherezade and Bakhtiyar are characters set within a frame narrative who attempt to save their lives by telling stories to a monarch who means to kill them. However, this is not the sole link between these two pieces of literature; characters from the *Bakhtiyar Nameh*, particularly King Azadbakht, also appear in the later *Arabian Nights* collection.

Persian myth's cultural roots are deep, going back more than five thousand years, stemming as they do from the original Aryan culture in its Indian homeland, which was later transplanted to and transformed on the Iranian Plateau. The Persian religious thought that grew out of ancient Aryan culture is rich in its own right and had important and lasting influences on Judaism, Christianity, and Islam. Persian sacred myth provides yet another fascinating look at how human beings have understood the structure of the universe and their place within it, while secular tales of heroes and kings allow one to escape into a land that is simultaneously mythical and historical, in which demons and dragons always get their comeuppance, and good always wins the day.

Section I: Religious Myths

The Myth of Yima

The myth of Yima is preserved in the Vendidad *section of the Zoroastrian holy text,* Zend-Avesta. *As with many other sections of the* Avesta, *this story is framed as a dialogue between the good god Ahura Mazda and the prophet Zarathustra. Yima's story functions both as a creation myth and a flood myth since once Yima has finished his work of enlarging the created world, Ahura Mazda tells him to save the people, plants, and animals from the coming apocalyptic winter. In addition, the story also sets up Zarathustra as a kind of successor to Yima since Yima initially refuses Ahura Mazda's call to be a lawgiver and a prophet, duties that are conferred upon Zarathustra at the very end of the myth. (In the retelling below, the myth is presented without the Zoroastrian framing.)*

In his work of enlarging the created world, Yima calls upon the power of the Spenta Armaiti. The six Spentas were manifestations of the power of Ahura Mazda, and each one had different qualities. The Spenta Armaiti was a feminine aspect of the divine and associated with religious devotion, devotion to the family, and the earth. The myth also references Vivahvant, an ancient Indo-Iranian sun deity (Vivasvat in India) who is said to be the father of Yima.

This myth mentions a place called Airyanem Vaejah, considered to be the ancient, original home of the Iranian people. Although in the Avesta, *Airyanem Vaejah takes on mythical qualities, it appears to have been a real place. Many theories have been advanced as to where Airyanem Vaejah actually was, and while scholars disagree on an exact location, many agree that Airyanem Vaejah probably was somewhere in central Asia, perhaps in what is now Afghanistan or Kazakhstan.*

When Ahura Mazda, the good god, had created the world and begun to people it, he went to Yima, the good shepherd, and said, "O Yima, son of Vivahvant, I, Ahura Mazda, ask you: Will you go among the people and teach them my religion?"

"O Ahura Mazda, I was not made for this task. I cannot teach the people your religion," said Yima.

"Very well," said Ahura Mazda. "If you will not be the teacher of my religion, then you will increase the world I have made, and you will enlarge it. You will be the protector and guardian of my world."

"That I will do gladly. I will be the protector and guardian of your world, and I will enlarge it and increase it. While I reign, there will be neither disease nor death, neither cold wind nor hot wind."

"It is well." Ahura Mazda gave Yima a golden seal and golden spear.

Yima ruled the world for three hundred years, and at the end of that time, Ahura Mazda looked down upon the earth and saw that it was full of herds and flocks, birds and dogs, and people and blazing red fires.

Ahura Mazda then went to Yima and said, "O Yima, son of Vivahvant, there is no more room in the world I have made."

So, Yima went forth to the south, following the path of the Sun.

He smote the earth with his golden seal and pierced it with his golden spear, saying, "O Spenta Armaiti, O Spirit of Holy Devotion, hear me! Open yourself! Stretch yourself! Make more room for herds and flocks, birds and dogs, people, and blazing red fires!"

Spenta Armaiti heard Yima's prayer, and the earth became larger than it had been by one third, and now there was more room for all the creatures.

Yima ruled over the world for six hundred years, and in that time, the world once again became full of herds and flocks, birds and dogs, and people and blazing red fires.

Ahura Mazda looked down and saw that the world he had created was full with no more room upon it, so Ahura Mazda then went to Yima and said, "O Yima, son of Vivahvant, there is no more room in the world I have made."

So, Yima went forth to the south, following the path of the Sun.

He smote the earth with his golden seal and pierced it with his golden spear, saying, "O Spenta Armaiti, O Spirit of Holy Devotion, hear me! Open yourself! Stretch yourself! Make more room for herds and flocks, birds and dogs, people, and blazing red fires!"

Spenta Armaiti heard Yima's prayer, and the earth became larger than it had been by two thirds, and now there was more room for all the creatures.

Yima ruled over the world for nine hundred years, and in that time, the world once again became full of herds and flocks, birds and dogs, and people and blazing red fires.

Ahura Mazda looked down and saw that the world he had created was full with no more room upon it, so Ahura Mazda then went to Yima and said, "O Yima, son of Vivahvant, there is no more room in the world I have made."

So, Yima went forth to the south, following the path of the Sun. He smote the earth with his golden seal and pierced it with his golden spear, saying, "O Spenta Armaiti, O Spirit of Holy Devotion, hear me! Open yourself! Stretch yourself! Make more room for herds and flocks, birds and dogs, people, and blazing red fires!"

Spenta Armaiti heard Yima's prayer, and the earth became larger than it had been by three thirds, and now there was more room for all the creatures.

There came a time when Ahura Mazda called together a council of all the good yazatas—the angels who do Ahura Mazda's will—and to this council also came Yima and all the best men of Airyanem Vaejah, through which flows the good Daiti River.

When all were assembled, Ahura Mazda said, "Hearken unto me, O Yima, the good shepherd of the earth! Winter is coming to the earth, and it will cover it with snow. This winter will kill two-thirds of the cattle, and when the snow melts, it will create rushing waters that will wash everything away.

"O Yima, son of Vivahvant, you must make a safe place for the people and the flocks, for the animals and the birds. Give that place four sides, and make each side the length of a stadium. Within this place bring the best of the people and the flocks. Let none be marred by disease or misfortune. Bring seeds of plants and crops and trees, bring dogs and birds. Bring red burning fires. Make a stream run through this place, and build dwellings and streets. In this place, let there be no strife and no enmity, no poverty and no disease, no spite and no falsehood. In this place, food will always be plentiful. Use the golden lance to shepherd all into this place, and then build a wall around it, with windows to give light."

Then Yima said, "O mighty Ahura Mazda, how am I to make this place according to your command?"

Ahura Mazda replied, "Trample the earth with your feet, and strike it with your hands, and the earth shall open up and provide the place to you."

Yima did as Ahura Mazda commanded. He made the safe place to be the length of a stadium on all four sides, and into that place, he brought the best of the people and the flocks, the seeds of plants and crops and trees, dogs and birds, and red burning fires. He built dwellings and streets, and in that place, there was neither strife nor enmity, neither poverty nor disease, neither spite nor falsehood, and food was always plentiful. Then, he built a wall around it and put windows into the wall to give light.

In this safe place that Yima made, there are also the Sun, Moon, and stars, and to those who dwell within this place, a year seems like a day. Every forty years, the people and the animals will give birth to twins, a boy and a girl, and all within this place live the very best of lives.

Angra Mainyu and Zarathustra

The nineteenth fargard (section or chapter) of the Avesta is dedicated to the tale of how Angra Mainyu and his demons attempted to kill Zarathustra but were forced to flee because of his holiness. This fargard also contains lists of invocations that are supposed to drive away evil forces and give detailed instructions for rituals of sacrifice and purification. (For this book, the lists of invocations have been truncated and the instructions concerning rituals omitted.)

This fargard also mentions the Saoshyant, whose name means "one who brings benefit." According to Zoroastrian belief, the Saoshyant will appear at the end of the world and rid creation of all evil, and he will come from Zarah Lake. However, another Zoroastrian belief states that there will be three Saoshyants, one for each three-thousand-year period of history, during which the struggle between Ahura Mazda and the forces of evil play out. The exact location of Zarah Lake is unknown, but some scholars place it in modern-day Afghanistan.

Out of the far north came Angra Mainyu, the Evil One, the king of the demons, and he said, "O Druj! Go you and smite the holy Zarathustra! Kill him!"

And so, the Druj, which is the demon Buiti, the demon of death, and a company of demons went to do Angra Mainyu's bidding.

When Zarathustra saw that the demons were there to kill him, he recited the Ahuna Vairya, the great prayer to Ahura Mazda.

The demons heard Zarathustra's prayer and fled in dismay.

The demons went to Angra Mainyu and said, "O tormenter! We cannot kill the holy Zarathustra. Death has no hold on him."

Zarathustra knew that the demons were plotting to kill him; he saw this within his soul. So, Zarathustra set out in search of Angra Mainyu, and on the way, he picked up many large stones, which were provided to him by the holy Ahura Mazda.

Angra Mainyu saw Zarathustra approaching with the great stones in his hands and said, "O Zarathustra, where are you going with those large stones in your hands?"

Zarathustra replied, "O Evil One! O Angra Mainyu! I am going to smite all your evil creations. I will smite the demons and the Nasu, the demon of rotting corpses. I will strike down idolatry. This I will do until the coming of the holy Saoshyant, who shall be born out of the waters of the Zarah Lake, who shall come out of the regions of the east."

"Do not smite my demons, O Zarathustra! Your father was Pourushaspa, and your mother worshiped me. Renounce the religion of Ahura Mazda and worship me instead, and I shall give you a great gift, one as great as the one I gave to Zahhak, and you shall become the ruler of nations!"

Zarathustra replied, "Never will I worship you, O Evil One! Never shall I turn aside from the true religion of Ahura Mazda, even though I must die for it."

"Very well. Then tell me: How will you smite my demons? How will you strike down idolatry? What words will you use? What will be your weapons?"

"My weapons are the mortar, the cup, and the sacred haoma drink. And my words are the words of Ahura Mazda. With those weapons and words, I will strike you down and smite your demons, for it is Ahura Mazda that brought the world into being. With the Amesha Spentas, he brought it into existence."

Then Zarathustra sang the Ahura Vairya, and when he was done, he addressed Ahura Mazda, saying, "O great and good Ahura Mazda! Instruct me! Tell me how I may defeat the Angra Mainyu and all his demons. Tell me how I may keep the Nasu from defiling the house of your faithful people. Tell me how I may cleanse those people who have become unclean and make them pure again."

Ahura Mazda replied, "I shall tell you how you may do this, and it is done by invocations.

"Invoke my good and holy religion.

"Invoke the Blessed Immortals, the Amesha Spentas who rule the seven regions of the world.

"Invoke the firmament of Heaven, the limitless time, and Vayu, who is the holy wind.

"Invoke the wind, and Spenta Armaiti, who watches over the earth.

"Invoke my *fravashi*, my holy essence, the holy essence of Ahura Mazda, the greatest and most blessed of all beings.

"Invoke all of creation, which I, Ahura Mazda, have made."

Then Zarathustra replied, saying, "I invoke all the creation that Ahura Mazda has made.

"I invoke Mithras, the victorious one who is armed with great weapons.

"I invoke the holy Sarosh, who wields a club to smite the demons.

"I invoke the holy word of Ahura Mazda.

"I invoke the firmament of Heaven, the limitless time, and Vayu, who is the holy wind.

"I invoke the wind, and Spenta Armaiti, who watches over the earth.

"I invoke the good religion of Ahura Mazda, which is the one true religion.

Then Zarathustra asked, "O great and good Ahura Mazda, how shall I make the sacrifice? How shall I purify those who are unclean?"

Ahura Mazda then gave Zarathustra many good instructions for making the sacrifice and purifying those who are unclean, and when this was done, Zarathustra praised Ahura Mazda and made many invocations that drive away all that is evil.

When Angra Mainyu and the demons saw the holy sacrifice Zarathustra had made and heard his invocations, they became deranged and ran to and fro.

Angra Mainyu shouted to all the demons, "Come and gather! Gather at the gates of Hell!"

The demons all shouted, "Let us gather at the gates of Hell!" and ran there screaming, "The holy Zarathustra, son of Pourushaspa, is born! He is the sword that smites us! He is the bane of all that is evil! He deprives us of our worship!"

Thus, did the demons flee from the holy words and acts of Zarathustra.

The Creation of the World

In addition to the Zend-Avesta, *Zoroastrian holy texts include the* Bundahisn, *a collection of religious writings in Middle Persian primarily having to do with cosmogony and cosmology. The* Bundahishn *was compiled in the ninth century and relates the history of creation and the battle between the good god Ohrmazd (Ahura Mazda) and the evil god Ahriman (Angra Mainyu). Two versions of the* Bundahisn *exist, the shorter Indian recension (or* Lesser Bundahisn*) and the longer Iranian recension (or* Greater Bundahisn*).*

As part of his act of creation, Ohrmazd creates six Blessed Immortals, which are avatars or manifestations of various aspects of Ohrmazd himself and many other divine spirits who aid the work of Ohrmazd and the Blessed Immortals. Of course, Ahriman does the same—although the beings he creates all share in his evil nature. Ohrmazd also regulates the division of the year, month, and day at the time of his creation, and the act of creation is effected through the performance of the sacred Yazishn ceremony, a complex ritual still performed today in Zoroastrian fire temples.

The version of the creation presented here has been condensed from the original found in the Greater Bundahisn, *which contains a great deal of repetition and religious and philosophical commentary interwoven into the relation of the events of the creation and the strife between Ohrmazd and Ahriman.*

In the beginning, even before the existence of time, Ohrmazd lived in regions of light. Ohrmazd was omniscient and perfectly good, and the regions of light in the heavens were his abode. In the regions of darkness lived Ahriman, and he was evil and inclined to destruction. Both the regions of light and darkness were limitless, and between them was the Void.

Now, because Ohrmazd was omniscient, he knew of the existence of Ahriman, even though their two abodes were separated from one another. Ohrmazd knew that whatever he created, Ahriman would try to destroy it, and so he first created beings that existed only in a spiritual state, unable to move, unable to think, with bodies that were spiritual and not solid. These beings remained in this state for three thousand years.

Ahriman knew nothing of these beings until he rose out of his abyss and crossed the Void into the regions of light. Ahriman saw the light, and he hated it. He vowed to destroy it, but when he tried to attack the light, he discovered that it was braver and more powerful than he was. Therefore, Ahriman fled back into his regions of darkness, where he created the devs, evil beings that shared Ahriman's malice and desire to destroy. Ahriman mustered his army of devs and with them assailed the regions of light.

When Ohrmazd saw the beings that Ahriman had created, he was repulsed, finding them corrupt and putrid. But when Ahriman saw the beings Ohrmazd had created, he found them beautiful and delightful, and he coveted them for himself.

Ohrmazd then said to Ahriman, "O Evil One! Listen to me! If you aid the beings that I have made, and if you offer worship, I will give immortality to you and the beings you have created."

Ahriman replied, "These things I will not do. I will not aid the beings you have made. I will not offer worship. I set myself forever against you and your creation. Whatever you create, I will turn away from you. Whatever you create, I will convince it to love me instead."

"You cannot destroy me, O Evil One, for you are not omnipotent. You may hold sway over my creatures for a time, but in the end, they will all return to me." Then Ohrmazd thought to himself that unless he set a limit on the contest between himself and Ahriman, it would go on forever, and without that limit, Ahriman would further be able to corrupt whatever Ohrmazd had made and take it for his own.

Therefore, Ohrmazd said to Ahriman, "Let us agree to limit the period of our strife against one another to nine thousand years."

Because Ahriman could not see the outcome of the battle as Ohrmazd could, Ahriman said, "It is well. I agree."

Now, Ohrmazd knew that these nine thousand years would pass thusly: In the first three thousand, there would be peace, and his own will would hold sway; in the second three thousand, there would be a mingling of the wills of Ohrmazd and Ahriman; and in the third three thousand, Ahriman would be defeated, and the creatures of Ohrmazd would live in peace.

Then Ohrmazd uttered the Ahuna Vairya and showed Ahriman the progress of their strife and its eventual ending with the destruction of the devs and the triumph of Ohrmazd and his creation. So, it was that when the Evil One heard the words of the Ahuna Vairya, he fell to his knees and returned to his regions of darkness so weakened that he did not rise again for three thousand years.

In this time before the creation of the world, Ohrmazd was not Lord. It was only after he made the world that his lordship existed. Before all other things, Ohrmazd created the yazads, those spirits who are the essence of goodness and whose creation enhanced the body and the lordship of Ohrmazd. The next thing Ohrmazd created was time. This he did because he knew that without time to impose a limit, the depredations of Ahriman would continue forever. In creating time, Ohrmazd knew that he was also making it possible for Ahriman to do his own evil works, but that without time, there also would be no end to Ahriman's destructive acts. And the duration of time from Ohrmazd's creation of the world to the final defeat of the Evil One is a span of twelve thousand years, and when that span is over, Ohrmazd's creation will join him and live with him forever in his dwelling where time is limitless.

When Ohrmazd made his creatures, he formed them out of light, making them out of fire, which is light and bright and can be seen from far off. But when Ahriman made his creatures, he formed them out of darkness, making them sinful, corrupt, and misshapen. Ohrmazd also made spirits to aid him in his creation, spirits that are manifestations of Ohrmazd and are part of him. The first of these spirits was Vohuman (Good Thought). The first of Ahriman's creatures was Mitokht (Falsehood), and the second was Akoman (Evil Thought).

Now, while Ahriman remained insensate in his abyss, Ohrmazd made the physical world.

First, Ohrmazd made the sky. He made it out of steel and diamond, and its crown touched the regions of endless light. Next Ohrmazd created water, and that water helped him create the wind and rain. Ohrmazd drew the earth out of the water, and at first, it was flat and featureless, but out of the earth, Ohrmazd caused the mountains to grow, and placed within them metals, gems, stone, and other good things that may be found beneath the earth.

After Ohrmazd created the mountains, he made the first tree. This tree grew in the very center of the earth, and it had neither bark nor branch nor thorn. It was the parent of all plants and had the life force of all plants contained within it. Once the tree was created, Ohrmazd then made the good animals.

On the bank of the river Daiti that ran through the middle of the earth, Ohrmazd created the Gav, the Holy Bull. The Gav was three rods high at the shoulder and as white and shining as the full moon. The water and plants that Ohrmazd created he gave to the Gav so that he might have health and strength. Upon the other side of the river, Ohrmazd created Gayomard, the father of the human race, and to Gayomard Ohrmazd he gave the gift of sleep.

In the sky, Ohrmazd placed the Sun and the Moon. He also fixed the stars in the firmament and shaped them into constellations. He made the twelve that are the Ram, the Bull, the Twins, the Crab, the Lion, the Virgin, the Balance, the Scorpion, the Centaur, the Capricorn, the Water Bearer, the Fish, and many more. He made the stars of different brightnesses and divided the sky and the year into twelve portions.

When the time comes for the last battle with Ahriman, the stars will descend from the heavens and fight on the side of Ohrmazd. In between earth and sky, Ohrmazd made clouds and wind. From the clouds came rain, and also lightning.

When Ohrmazd created the world, he did so with the aid of six Blessed Immortals, and together with the most holy Ohrmazd, there are seven Blessed Immortals. Together with Ohrmazd, the Blessed Immortals do battle with evil forces, and the Blessed Immortals are both themselves and reflections of Ohrmazd.

The first of the Blessed Immortals is Ohrmazd himself, and for himself, he took the human beings of the world. The second Blessed Immortal is Vohuman, and for himself, he took all the good animals. Ardwahisht (Best Truth) is the third Blessed Immortal, and for himself, he took fire. The fourth Blessed Immortal is Shahrewar (Desirable Dominion), and for himself, he took metal. Spandarmad (Holy Devotion) is the fifth Blessed Immortal, and for herself, she took the earth. Hordad (Wholeness) is the sixth Blessed Immortal, and for herself, she took water. The seventh Blessed Immortal is Amurdad (Immortality), and for herself, she took the plants. With the aid of other divine spirits, the Blessed Immortals protect the world and keep it in existence.

According to the will of Ohrmazd, each day is divided into five segments: Morning, midday, evening, ablution time, and dawn. Each segment has a divine spirit to watch over it. Ohrmazd made these divisions because prior to the world's creation, all was illuminated by an eternal midday.

Ohrmazd created the world while performing the holy Yazishn ceremony with the Blessed Immortals. This he did in the Rapithwin Gah, the midday time of the day.

When the ceremony was over, and all had been created, Ohrmazd turned to the *farohars* of the human beings, the aspect of the soul that is always in the presence of Ohrmazd, and said, "I give you a choice: You can assume a material form and thus strive against the Druj, the demon whose power is of corruption and death, so that you may conquer the Druj and thus enter into eternal life, perfect, deathless, and without an adversary. Or, do you want me to protect you forever from the forces of evil?"

The farohars knew that Ahriman and his demons would be conquered in the end, so they agreed to take on material bodies and thus live in the world Ohrmazd had made until the time came when they might regain their bodies and become perfect and immortal.

Now, when Ahriman became aware of the creations of Ohrmazd, he roused from his stupor, along with all the demons he had created, attacked first the sky, trying to pull it down and drag it under the earth, and all became as dark as night. Ahriman and his demons attacked the waters, sullying them and making them impure. He released upon the Earth all manner of vile creatures—dragons, serpents, toads, stinging insects, and many other kinds of venomous and noxious things so that no place on the Earth was free of them. Ahriman went to the first tree and poisoned it so that it withered and died. He went to the Gav and Gayomard and loosed upon them all manner of vices and suffering. This is how greed, poverty, disease, hunger, and other ills came into the world.

When Ohrmazd saw that Ahriman would attack the Gav, he gave him healing medicine to protect him and relieve his suffering. But even with that medicine, the Gav became feeble and died. To protect Gayomard, Ohrmazd cast him into a deep sleep, and when Gayomard awoke, he found the world plunged into the deepest darkness. The stars were at war with the demons, and all of creation was thrown into chaos.

Seeing the things that Ohrmazd had made now in disarray, Ahriman next attacked Gayomard. Ahriman sent Astwihad, the demon of death, and a thousand other demons to slay him, but no matter how they tried, they could not kill Gayomard, for the time of his death had not yet arrived.

Gayomard said, "Now that the Evil One has awakened and come to disturb the Earth, human beings shall arise from my seed and populate the world, and they shall do many good deeds."

Ahriman next went to the fire, sullying it with smoke and darkness. The planets and constellations fought with the demons of Ahriman, and for ninety days, the angels of Heaven fought with the demons of Ahriman, until finally Ahriman and all his minions were defeated and thrown into Hell, which is at the center of the world.

Section II: Bakhtiyar Nameh

Bakhtiyar Nameh *is a collection of stories compiled by Persian author Sams-al-Din Mohammad Daqayeqi Marvazi around the turn of the seventh century. The collection includes nine tales that are sandwiched within a frame story that tells the history of Prince Bakhtiyar, from his birth and abandonment by his royal parents to his eventual reunion with his family as a young adult. Thus, the frame story participates in the common folklore trope of the foundling prince, while the central stories each revolve around different topics.*

The frame story in Bakhtiyar Nameh *is set in the provinces of Sistan and Kirman. In ancient times, Sistan covered the region that now includes parts of Eastern Iran and Western Afghanistan on either side of the Helmand River, while Kirman is in South-central Iran. Tales involving Bakhtiyar's father, Azadbakht, also appear in the Arab collection known as* The Thousand and One Nights *or* The Arabian Nights.

The entire Bakhtiyar Nameh *is too long to be presented here in its entirety, so only the frame story and two of the internal tales are retold below.*

The Birth of Bakhtiyar

There was a time when the country of Sistan was ruled by a king named Azadbakht, who had a vizier named Sipehsalar. Sipehsalar was a man of great strength and skill. When he wielded his scimitar, even the Moon hid herself for fear of it.

Sipehsalar had a daughter, who was the most beautiful young woman in the whole kingdom, with jet-black hair perfumed with all the spices of Arabia. The most perfect red rose would look gray and wan next to Sipehsalar's daughter, who outshone all others as the noonday Sun does the Moon.

Sipehsalar loved his daughter excessively, to the point where he could not bear to be more than an hour without her. Now, there came a time when Sipehsalar had to go on a tour of inspection of the countryside, to see what state the kingdom was in and how her people were faring, and to ensure that the governors who ruled the various provinces were executing their offices justly. The journey dragged on and on, and soon Sipehsalar found himself becoming distraught over the amount of time he was spending away from his home and his family. Therefore, he summoned two messengers and sent them to his home to fetch his daughter and bring her to her father so that she might accompany him on the remainder of his journey.

The messengers rushed back to the capital city in haste. They went to Sipehsalar's house and told the young woman that her father desired that she join him as he toured the country. She assented to the request and, after packing the things that would be needful to her, got into the palanquin that had been readied to convey her to the place where her father was lodged.

It happened that while the messengers and Sipehsalar's daughter were on their way to meet her father, King Azadbakht was riding toward them on his way back to the city after having spent the day hunting.

When the king approached, the messengers dismounted their horses and prostrated themselves on the ground before him, saying, "May God save you, O king, and grant you a long and prosperous life."

"You are the messengers of Sipehsalar, yes? When you rejoin him, please give him my greetings and tell him I await with great interest the results of his inspection," said the king.

The messengers promised to do as the king bid them the moment they were again in Sipehsalar's presence.

The king then resumed his journey back home, but just as he passed the palanquin, a passing breeze lifted the curtain, revealing the lovely young woman seated inside. The king caught sight of Sipehsalar's daughter, and immediately his heart was inflamed with the most ardent love.

The king turned to the attendants who had accompanied him on the hunt and said, "Accompany this young woman back to the city, and see that she is lodged in the greatest comfort in my palace." Then Azadbakht said to the messengers, "I give you a new task: Return to Sipehsalar and tell him that I intend to make his daughter my wife and hope to be worthy of her and my father-in-law-to-be."

The Sipehsalar's messengers again prostrated themselves and said, "O great king, may God grant you a long life and riches beyond measure! May your throne be a light to the world, and your words ever wise! Sipehsalar surely will count himself the most fortunate of fathers. We ask that you allow us to conduct Sipehsalar's daughter to her father. There we will tell him your will so that he might have time to prepare for the wedding, as befits your royal majesty."

"What? Would you dare defy me? No, you shall go to Sipehsalar as I have commanded you, and I shall accompany his daughter back to the city myself." The king badly wanted to punish the messengers for their temerity, but he stayed his hand because he did not want Sipehsalar's daughter to think him cruel.

The messengers went on their way to bring the king's news to Sipehsalar, and the king and his retinue returned to the city with Sipehsalar's daughter, who was taken to the women's quarters, where she was received with great honor.

In the morning, King Azadbakht summoned all his chief advisers and the chief judges of his kingdom.

"I intend to marry the daughter of Vizier Sipehsalar, and I desire to know your thoughts on the matter," he said.

One and all, the advisers and judges told the king that it was a most auspicious match and preparations for the wedding should begin at once. To this end, they drew up a decree announcing the marriage and ceremonies that were to be held to solemnize it. The king then dictated a letter announcing his marriage and bid his secretaries make many copies that could be brought to all corners of his realm, so his people might know his happiness and rejoice with him. To Sipehsalar, the king wrote with his own hand, saying how honored he felt to have such a bride and hoping that Sipehsalar would bless the union and rejoice along with him.

When Sipehsalar received the king's letter, he felt anything but joy. Rather, he wept bitter tears to know that his beloved daughter would be taken from him and made the king's bride. Sipehsalar's tears were not just for sorrow; no, they were also tears of anger, for the king had not even had the decency to allow Sipehsalar's daughter to see her father one last time before being whisked away, nor had he had the decency to ask for the young woman's hand before publishing the marriage decree.

However, Sipehsalar had served the king for many years, and he was a man of wisdom and diplomacy. He wrote a response to the king that outwardly spoke of his gladness at having such a splendid son-in-law, and of his hope that the union would be a long and happy one, but in his heart, Sipehsalar was plotting revenge. There were many months yet left in his tour of inspection, and he vowed to use them well to sow seeds of distrust and sedition against the king and rally the powerful men of the kingdom to his own side.

Finally, Sipehsalar deemed his plans were ripe, and he summoned all the generals of the army to a council. First, he made the generals swear an oath of secrecy, and then he made sure that each of them would be willing to support whatever thing Sipehsalar told them needed to be done.

The generals took the oath and assured Sipehsalar of their loyalty, whereupon Sipehsalar said, "You have heard of the dastardly way King Azadbakht took my daughter to wife. He snatched her from the road like a brigand and rode back to the palace with her as though she were a piece of loot. What did I do to deserve this insult? I have only given him my loyal service from the very first day, but he rides off with my daughter without so much as a by-your-leave."

The generals all agreed that the king had used Sipehsalar very ill and asked what he required of them.

"Gather all your men. Arm them. And when all is ready, we attack Azadbakht and depose him like the cur he is," said Sipehsalar.

The Sipehsalar opened up his treasury and paid vast sums of money to the generals so that they might ready their armies for an assault on Azadbakht.

It took very little time to muster the army and march to Azadbakht's capital city, and even less time for the army to breach the walls and fan out through the streets, which they did in the dead of night.

Azadbakht was roused from sleep by the cries of those being slain and the clash of arms. He looked out the window and saw that his city was being attacked from all sides.

"What shall we do?" Azadbakht asked of his queen. "This army will have taken the city before dawn, and they will have my head on a pike at the gate soon thereafter."

"Let us fly as quickly as may be. Surely there is some other friendly prince who will welcome us in our time of need," said the queen.

Azadbakht agreed that this was the wisest course, and so he and the queen quickly prepared to travel to the kingdom of Kirman, whose ruler had always been on good terms with Azadbakht. The king ordered that horses be saddled. Then he put on his armor and girt on his sword before taking a great store of gems and gold from the treasury so that he and the queen might buy what was needful in their flight. Once the king and queen were mounted on their horses, they made their way to a secret underground passage that led out of the city and into the desert.

The king and queen traveled for the rest of the night and throughout the following day. They were weary and thirsty, but they went on until they arrived at a well that seemed to promise water. When the king drew some of the water, he found that it was brackish and foul and in no way fit to drink. But this was not the end of their troubles: The queen had been with child for the nine months prior, and the fear and hardship of their journey brought on her labor pains.

"My husband, leave this place and search for water. My pains are upon me, and it would not be meet for the king to die of thirst like a commoner if water were available nearby. My own life matters not. Save yourself, for you are the king," said the queen.

"That I will not do, for nothing in this world is dearer to me than my beloved wife. I would gladly set aside my throne and all my riches to keep you by my side. No, we stay together, for I do not know how I would live without you," said Azadbakht,

It was then that the queen cried out, and soon she gave birth to a baby boy. The child was exquisitely beautiful, surpassing even the Moon in the fairness of his features. The queen cradled him to her breast and began to nurse him as a mother should.

"My dearest wife, do not become attached to the child. We cannot take him with us. We have not enough food or water to support the three of us. We must leave him behind and hope that God will send good people to his aid, who will love him and raise him as their own," said the king.

The king then took his newborn son and wrapped him in a cloth that was richly embroidered with gold. He then put a bracelet made of ten large pearls about the child's neck. With hearts full of anguish, the king and queen mounted their horses and rode away, all the while commending their infant son to the care of the Almighty.

When Azadbakht and his queen arrived at the principal city of Kirman, the King of Kirman sent out musicians and servants to welcome his guests and conduct them in great honor to his palace. The King of Kirman commanded a great banquet to be held and sent his son and two other servants to wait upon Azadbakht and the queen, to see that they lacked for nothing.

The banquet was a splendid affair, with all manner of good food and good wine, and delightful music played by the palace musicians. Although Azadbakht was most grateful for the king's hospitality, nothing could assuage his grief over his son and the loss of his kingdom, and he could not hide his tears.

"Why do you weep, O my guest, who is most welcome of all to my house? Behold, here is a feast in your honor and music to delight you. What reason have you to mourn?" asked the King of Kirman.

"O my most royal host, truly your hospitality is without stint and compare. But I cannot rejoice when my kingdom has been taken from me, and an enemy sits upon my throne," said Azadbakht.

The King of Kirman then bade Azadbakht tell his whole tale, and when the king had heard all, he felt deep compassion toward his guest. He ordered his musicians and servants to divert Azadbakht and his queen all day, to help keep their minds from their sorrows.

In the morning, he mustered his army.

The King of Kirman said to Azadbakht, "Behold, O my most royal guest, I have mustered my army for you. I bid you lead it to your capital, and so depose the usurper to your throne."

Azadbakht thanked the King of Kirman most gratefully and then led the army back to Sistan.

When Sipehsalar saw Azadbakht approaching at the head of a mighty army, he fled in fear, while the people of Sistan bowed down before Azadbakht and begged his forgiveness and mercy.

Azadbakht pardoned them, one and all, and ascended his throne, from where he ruled with great justice and mercy. He paid the King of Kirman's soldiers most generously and then sent them back to Kirman, laden with many precious gifts to give their king.

The kingdom of Sistan was peaceful and prosperous under Azadbakht's rule, but the king and the queen could never forget their tiny son, whom they had abandoned at that lonely well in the desert. Both of them were convinced that he must have been devoured by wild beasts soon after they left him, and for all the success of Azadbakht's reign, their hearts were ever heavy and in mourning for their dear son.

Bakhtiyar and the Bandits

Little did Azadbakht and his queen know that not long after they had ridden away from the well, a band of robbers rode up, having heard the wails of the infant. The robbers' leader was named Firokh Suvar, and when he picked up the crying child, he was taken by the infant's great beauty.

"Look at this child," he said to his followers. "Surely, he is the son of some great and powerful person. See how beautiful he is? And look, he is wrapped in a cloth of gold, and has a bracelet of ten pearls around his neck."

"What will you do with him?" asked one of the robbers.

"I will keep him and raise him as my own. I have no child, and I have longed for one. We will take him with us, and we will call him Khodadad."

Firokh took the infant to his home, where he found a wet nurse to tend him. The boy grew and flourished under the care of Firokh and the nurse, and when he was old enough, Firokh taught him all the things a man ought to know, such as horsemanship and the wielding of arms. So strong and clever was the boy that by the time he was fifteen years old, even an army of five hundred men could not stand against him.

Firokh loved Khodadad very deeply and took the boy with him everywhere he went. However, Khodadad refused to help his father and his band of robbers to plunder a caravan. Khodadad felt sorry for the people of the caravan, and he found banditry distasteful.

Firokh agreed that Khodadad need not participate in the attack but insisted that he go along and wait nearby until the looting was done.

One day, Firokh led his band out to attack a nearby caravan, and, as was usual, Khodadad went with them but waited to the side while the bandits did their work. However, this time, Firokh and his band were outnumbered, and the men of the caravan fought back with such ferocity that many of the robbers were killed and many others were taken prisoner. During the battle, Firokh was wounded and was just about to be taken prisoner when Khodadad came charging in to his rescue. Khodadad fought bravely and was near to rescuing Firokh when he fell from his horse and was taken prisoner himself. Khodadad, Firokh, and the other robbers who had been captured were put into chains and marched to the capital city of Sistan, where they were brought before King Azadbakht for judgment.

Now, when Azadbakht looked upon Khodadad, his heart welled up with love, for he thought, *Surely the infant I abandoned at the well would be a youth such as this, were he still alive!*

Then Azadbakht said to Khodadad, "Step forward and tell me your name."

"O most royal sovereign, my name is Khodadad."

"Why is it that a youth with such strength and beauty as yours should plunder a caravan and steal things belonging to others, things to which you have no right?"

Khodadad replied, "O most royal sovereign, it is true that I was there, but it is false that I stole anything from anyone, and God himself sees my innocence."

Azadbakht pardoned Khodadad then and there and ordered that his chains be removed.

Then he gave the boy his own cloak and said, "No more shall you be called Khodadad. From today forth, you shall be known as Bakhtiyar, and fortune shall be your friend from henceforth."

Then Azadbakht said to the captured robbers, "I grant you pardon on two conditions. One is that you never again engage in banditry. The other is that you enter into my service. If you do both those things, you will be rewarded generously."

The robbers agreed, and from that time forward, they served the king, and caravans passed through the country of Sistan unmolested.

Azadbakht put Bakhtiyar in charge of the royal stables, and so well did the youth discharge his duties that soon all the horses were sleek and fat. When the king asked how his horses had prospered so well, he was told that Bakhtiyar's attendance upon them was the reason.

Azadbakht then sent for Bakhtiyar and said, "You have managed my stables so very well that I think you might be entrusted with something of greater importance. Here are the keys to my treasury. You are now the keeper of my treasure."

Bakhtiyar prostrated himself before Azadbakht and promised to do his utmost to discharge his duties with honesty and discretion.

In managing the king's treasury, Bakhtiyar proved himself to be just as adept at keeping the horses. Azadbakht soon came to rely on the young man's good advice, and in time, the king would not hold audiences with any person unless Bakhtiyar could be there to advise him.

The Ten Viziers

Now, Azadbakht also had ten viziers who served him. These viziers had seen the rise of Bakhtiyar in the king's esteem, and they burned with envy. Therefore, they held counsel together and agreed that they would look for an opportunity to accomplish Bakhtiyar's fall from favor, and even his death, if at all possible.

The viziers watched and waited, and finally, their patience was rewarded when one night, Bakhtiyar spent the night drinking in the treasury. He drank so much wine that he was nearly insensible, and when he exited the treasury with the intent of going to his quarters, he instead became lost and wandered through the palace until he arrived at the king's bedchamber. Bakhtiyar opened the door and saw a sort of throne, and many cushions and hangings of silk in a room lit by many candles. Seeing only a comfortable room, and feeling the wine's effects, Bakhtiyar went inside, sat down upon the throne, and promptly fell asleep. Some time later, Azadbakht entered the chamber, thinking to take his rest. He was furious to find Bakhtiyar sitting on his chair, fast asleep.

"How dare you enter my private apartments! Explain yourself at once!" shouted the king.

Bakhtiyar was still heavily intoxicated, so the only effect the king's shouts had was to rouse Bakhtiyar from sleep enough that he fell off the chair. But even then, he was too insensible to realize his peril; instead, he simply rolled underneath the throne and went back to sleep.

Azadbakht then called for servants to remove Bakhtiyar, put him in chains, and throw him into the dungeon. The king then drew his sword and strode into the women's quarters, where he demanded that the queen explain how Bakhtiyar was found in the royal bedchamber.

"O my king and O my husband, I have no knowledge of this," said the queen.

"Spare me your lies. There is no way he could have found his way into that chamber without your help."

"O my king, I say to you that I have no knowledge of this, and if you wish proof of my innocence, keep me confined here until you can establish the truth of the matter."

In the morning, Azadbakht summoned the ten viziers. He told them what had transpired the night before and asked their advice on what should be done.

One vizier realized that this was the chance he and his fellows had waited for, and so he said, "What did you expect, O my king and O my royal master, when you brought into your service a low-born churl who furthermore had been raised by brigands? I had my doubts about him from the first but held my tongue because your glorious majesty seemed so taken with the boy. But now his true nature has manifested itself, and you must punish him accordingly."

Azadbakht then commanded that Bakhtiyar be brought before him.

When the young man was stood before the king in his chains, Azadbakht said, "What have you to say for yourself? I, for one, think you the most ungrateful wretch in my entire kingdom. I raised you to high office and entrusted you with vital duties, but in the end, you betrayed me by sneaking into my private apartments. Speak! Explain yourself!"

"O my king and O my royal master, I truly am grateful for all that you have given me, and all I have to say for myself is that I have no memory of how I arrived in your apartments. I beg your majesty's forgiveness and mercy for what I did since I knew not what I was doing and meant no harm," said Bakhtiyar.

Then the first vizier requested the king's permission to go to the women's quarters and inquire as to what the queen knew of these events, and Azadbakht gave his assent.

The vizier went before the queen and said, "O my queen, you surely know of the entrance of Bakhtiyar into the royal chambers last night, and you surely know that the king accuses you of having given him entrance. His majesty is greatly wroth with you, and the only way that you can save yourself from his vengeance is to tell him that Bakhtiyar entered the royal quarters with the intent to ravish you and with the intent to do away with the king and steal his throne. If you say this, the king will have mercy on you and execute Bakhtiyar for his crimes. It is the only way to save yourself."

The queen was astonished at this advice and said, "How can I say that when I know it not to be true? I will not be the cause of an innocent man's death."

"Bakhtiyar is not an innocent man, my lady. Before he rose in the king's favor, he was a brigand among brigands, and your statement will merely restore to him the fate that should have been his long ago."

The vizier made these and many other arguments until finally, the queen gave in and agreed to testify against Bakhtiyar with the words the vizier told her to say.

After hearing the queen's testimony, the king ordered that Bakhtiyar be returned to the prison in chains, where he was to await the most terrifying punishment the king could bestow upon him. Bakhtiyar was duly thrown into the dungeon, and the viziers went to their homes rejoicing that their time of vengeance had come at last and thinking of ways they might induce the king to execute the young man sooner rather than later.

Bakhtiyar's First Story: The Tale of the Unfortunate Merchant

On the following day, the second vizier stood before the king and said, "O most gracious majesty, may you have a long life, and may your reign shine forever! I have come to ask you to execute Bakhtiyar without delay since it is vital that your majesty not be seen as weak and vacillating."

"Very well. But first, have him brought here so that I may tell him his fate," said the king.

Accordingly, Bakhtiyar was taken from the prison and soon stood before the king in his chains.

"You are here so that I may pronounce sentence upon you, for it is my wish that your death be made an example for all others who might harbor ill thoughts against me or my household," said Azadbakht.

"O mighty sovereign, may God grant you long life and limitless victories over your enemies. I know it to be my duty to try and save myself from the gallows since I know myself to be innocent, and since God knows this also. But unfortunately, I share the plight of the merchant who was ceaselessly plagued by misfortune, such that everything he attempted went awry," said Bakhtiyar.

"I do not know this tale. Tell it to me now."

"As your majesty wishes. Here is the tale . . . A merchant once lived in the city of Basrah, and this merchant was immensely wealthy. But no matter what business or trade he attempted, it invariably came to naught. Because of this, it did not take long before all his wealth was sorely depleted, and he was on the verge of ruin.

"When the merchant saw how little of his money was left, he decided to invest it in a store of grain, which he intended to keep until the following year so that he might sell it at a profit. He duly bought the grain and stored it in a granary, but the following year, the harvest was better than usual, and as a result, the price of grain fell. Therefore, the merchant decided to keep his grain in storage and wait to see what the following year might bring. But that winter, there was so much rain that the city flooded, including the storehouse where the merchant kept his grain, and so the grain rotted and had to be thrown away.

"After some time spent mourning this misfortune, the merchant decided to sell his house and join a company of merchants, who were sailing to a far land in hopes of finding fortune there. But on the journey, a storm blew up and wrecked the ship. Many of those aboard drowned, but the merchant was among those lucky few who managed to cling to a plank and drifted onto land.

"Hungry and thirsty, his clothes in tatters, the merchant wandered inland. He had walked some miles through a desert when he saw a man in the distance. The merchant's spirits rose, for where one man was, others might be, and perhaps there would be someone who could help him. So, the merchant walked toward the man and soon saw that there was a village nearby. The chief of the village, or dikhan, had made himself a little summer house just outside the village, and he happened to be there when the merchant arrived, and so saw the poor, tattered wretch. The dikhan then told his servants to fetch the man and bring him into the summer house, where the dikhan inquired as to what had happened to the merchant and made him comfortable with food and drink. The dikhan was so moved by the merchant's tale of woe that he gave the merchant some of his clothes and bid him stay as his guest until his fortunes could be reversed.

"The dikhan placed the merchant in charge of his fields of grain, saying that when the harvest came in, the merchant might have an eleventh share of it to be his. The merchant was pleased and grateful and worked diligently to see that the crops were properly tended. All his diligence paid off, for when the harvest came in, it proved more than usually abundant.

"The merchant did an accounting of the harvest and discovered that the share promised to him by the dikhan was quite substantial.

Surely, he never meant to give me this much, thought the merchant. *What if he chooses not to keep his word?*

Therefore, the merchant took an eleventh share of the grain and hid it away, thinking to restore it to the dikhan if he indeed kept his promise. The merchant hid that eleventh share of grain in a nearby cave, but it was discovered by a thief, who stole it all away.

"When the dikhan made his accounting of the harvest, he set aside an eleventh share for the use of the merchant. The merchant then confessed that he had doubted the dikhan's honesty and had already hidden an eleventh share in a cave. The dikhan duly sent some of his servants to recover that store of grain, but when they got to the cave, they found that it had disappeared. They returned in haste to the dikhan and told him what they had seen, whereupon the dikhan turned to the merchant and said, 'Ungrateful wretch! Not only would you doubt my word after all my help, but you would lose me a full eleventh share of a fine harvest! Begone! You leave as you came, with nothing. Do not return to my village ever again.'

"The merchant left the village and headed toward the seashore, mourning his misfortune and wondering how he might save himself. When he arrived at the shore, he came across six men from the village who were pearl divers. The merchant and the men knew one another, and when the divers asked why the merchant was so downcast, he told them his whole sorry tale.

"'Oh, that is so unfortunate,' said one of the divers. 'We surely must help you. We will bring you whatever we find the next time we dive for pearls, to restore your fortunes.'

"And so, the divers accordingly dove into the water, and each one brought up a beautiful pearl and gave it to the merchant. The merchant was most grateful, and he went on his way with a merry heart, thinking of all the ways he might use the pearls to increase his fortune.

"Along the road, the merchant was soon overtaken by a band of robbers, who happened to be going the same direction. Desiring not to lose what little fortune he now had, the merchant put three of the pearls into his mouth and concealed the rest among his clothing. At first, the robbers did not bother the merchant, but at one point, he decided to speak to them, and one of the pearls came out of his mouth. When the robbers saw this, they threatened the merchant with great violence if he did not give him the rest. The merchant accordingly gave them the other two pearls in his mouth but kept the rest concealed. Placated, the robbers went on their way, and the merchant thanked the Almighty that at least he still had half his treasure to do with as he would.

"The merchant continued on his journey, but because he could not afford a room in an inn, he was forced to sleep in a nearby barn. This, combined with his long journey on the road, had disarranged and dirtied his clothing so that when he arrived at the shop of the jeweler, where he intended to sell the pearls, the jeweler looked askance at him. The merchant brought out the pearls that he wished to sell and asked what the jeweler might be willing to pay. The jeweler was astonished that such large magnificent pearls would be in the possession of such a rag-tag person as the merchant.

"'How did you come by these pearls?' asked the jeweler.

"'My friends gave them to me as a parting gift,' said the merchant.

"'A likely story. Perhaps you stole them from my shop and are now trying to swindle me.'

"'Most assuredly, I am telling the truth.'

But the jeweler would not believe him, no matter how much the merchant protested, and soon the two men were engaged in a violent squabble that drew the attention of others in the marketplace. The jeweler was a man of some repute in the town, and so his story was believed over that of the merchant. Word of the argument came to the king, who pronounced the merchant guilty. The pearls were given to the jeweler, and the merchant was taken away to prison to await sentencing.

"Now, it happened that a few days after the merchant was imprisoned, the divers who had given him the pearls came to the city. They decided to go to the prison to distribute alms, and there they found their friend, bound in chains. When they asked the merchant what had happened, he related the whole sad tale. The pearl divers were outraged and went immediately to the king's court, where they explained the situation and vouched for the merchant's innocence, with the result that the merchant was freed and the jeweler brought before the king to explain himself. When the jeweler could offer no defense for his actions, the king pronounced him guilty and executed him for bringing false witness against a stranger. The king then turned the jeweler's shop and other property over to the merchant to be his in recompense for what he had unjustly suffered. He then ordered the merchant to be given a fine set of clothes and a hot bath and made the merchant the overseer of the royal treasury.

"The merchant served the king most diligently and was rewarded accordingly. This roused the envy of one of the king's viziers, who began to look for a means by which he might cause the merchant's downfall.

"Now, the king's daughter had a summer house next to the treasury, where she would spend a few days from time to time as it pleased her. A mouse had made a hole in the wall that divided the treasury from the summer house's grounds. One day, the merchant needed to drive a nail into the wall, and he, unfortunately, hit upon the mouse's nest, such that when the nail went into the wall, it went quite through and knocked out one of the bricks on the summer house side, creating a good-sized hole. The merchant saw what had happened and blocked up the hole with some clay.

"The vizier happened to see the merchant applying the clay to the wall and decided that this was his chance to rid himself of his rival. He accordingly went to the king and said that he had seen the merchant drive a nail into the wall and knock out a brick on the other side so that he could spy on the king's daughter and that the merchant had stoppered the hole with clay in an attempt to conceal his crime. The king was outraged at this and stormed down to the treasury, where he saw the merchant with dirty hands, having just finished applying the last of the wet clay.

"The king believed what the vizier said, despite the merchant's protestations of innocence and his explanation of what had actually happened. The king then ordered the merchant's eyes to be scooped out and his person to be set outside the palace gate. The king then went to the summer house to see to his daughter's welfare, only to be told that she had not been there for some days since she had decided to spend her time in another part of the palace. After hearing this, the king went to the treasury and removed the clay from the hole, which he saw had indeed been the work of a mouse. He also saw that the brick had been dislodged by accident and that the merchant had been both honest and trustworthy. The king, therefore, ordered the vizier to be severely punished and deeply lamented and regretted that he had not taken the time to investigate before ordering the merchant's fate.

"Therefore, your majesty," said Bakhtiyar, having completed his tale, "we see how the king might have prevented both his distress and that of the merchant had he but taken the time to understand what had truly happened, and not made a judgment in anger. If your majesty pleases, be not hasty in your judgment, to avoid the fate of that king. Give me some more time to prove my innocence."

Azadbakht was impressed by Bakhtiyar's story and duly agreed to give him another day's respite. He ordered that Bakhtiyar be taken back to prison and postponed the execution for the time being.

Bakhtiyar's Last Story: The Tale of the King of Persia

Day after day, Bakhtiyar was brought before the king, and each day one of the viziers, in turn, would make the case for Bakhtiyar's execution. But day after day, Bakhtiyar begged mercy of the king and won a stay of execution by telling the king a lively tale.

This went on for nine days, and on the tenth day, the tenth vizier sent a message to the queen that said, "O my queen, well you know that the brigand Bakhtiyar has been sentenced to death, but every day he manages to gain himself time by means of tales. I implore you to speak to your royal husband and demand that this farce is put to an end and the criminal executed without delay."

The queen did as the vizier asked. She spoke to the king before he left the royal apartments, and with his wife's persuasion, he agreed that today indeed, Bakhtiyar would meet his end. The king then went into the council chamber, where the viziers were already waiting for him.

Before the tenth vizier could rise to make his case, the king said, "I have decided that we must put an end to this farce. Today Bakhtiyar will be executed."

Then the king commanded that Bakhtiyar be brought into the chamber, and when he arrived, the king said, "For nine days now you have protested your innocence, but we have seen not one bit of evidence that you are telling the truth. Today indeed shall you be executed, for I have made the decree."

Bakhtiyar began to weep when he heard this and said, "I know that I am innocent, and have used my tales as a way to gain myself time in the hopes that somehow I might escape this fate. But now I see that this fate is indeed what God has in store for me, and I will not fight against my destiny as did the King of Persia, for I have no more hope of success than did he."

Azadbakht said, "I have not heard this tale of the King of Persia. I bid you tell it to me."

"As your most gracious majesty commands. Here is my tale: Once there was a King of Persia, who was mighty and wealthy, but he was unhappy because he had no child. He prayed and prayed that God might give him a son, and at length, one of the women of his household was found with child. The king was overjoyed that, at last, he might have a son and an heir, but that night he had a strange dream. In the dream, an old man said to him, 'God has given you a son, but his life will be short and his end tragic. When the child reaches his seventh year, a lion shall seize him and carry him to the top of a mountain, then throw him down the side, and the child shall roll to the bottom all covered in blood and earth.'

"The king was much troubled by this dream and asked his wisest viziers what it meant and what might be done about it, but all they could say was, 'If this is the fate God has decreed, then who are you to think it might be turned aside?' The king would not be dissuaded and said that he would indeed struggle against this fate even if it were the Almighty himself who decreed it.

"Some days later, one of the king's viziers drew up a horoscope for the king in which he saw that the king would be killed by his own son twenty years hence. The vizier went to the king to inform him of what he had found, and the king said, 'If you have spoken falsehood, you shall forfeit your life.'

"In the meantime, the king ordered that an underground chamber be constructed to hold his son and the boy's nurse, as proof against the doom predicted by the dream. The nurse and the child lived there for seven years, and at the end of the seventh year, a lion found its way into the chamber, where it devoured the nurse and then snatched up the child. The lion brought the child to the top of a mountain and then released him, whereupon the child rolled to the bottom, where he lay half-dead, covered in blood and earth.

"Not long thereafter, one of the king's secretaries happened to ride by that place and found the child, who was badly wounded but still alive. The secretary took the child into his home, where he treated the boy like one of his own children and taught him his trade. Meanwhile, the king had gone to the underground chamber to see whether his dream had come true. Finding the chamber deserted, he assumed that the nurse had run away with the child, and so he ordered messengers to go throughout the land to find her and the child, but they always returned without success.

"Time passed, and soon the king's son had attained the age of thirteen years, at which time his foster father determined that he was sufficiently schooled and trustworthy to accompany him to his employment within the palace. The king often saw the secretary and his young assistant, and each time he looked upon the youth, he felt an increase in his affection for the lad, until one day he told the secretary that he would like to take the boy into his service. The secretary assented with many thanks since serving the king was a great honor not usually accorded to one so young. To the young man, the king gave the office of armor-bearer and the duty to attend upon the king's person.

"The young man served his king with great distinction for many years, until one day the kingdom of Persia was beset by an enemy, who had mustered a powerful army and marched upon the capital with the intent of sacking it and taking the throne away from the king. The King of Persia gathered his troops and went to the field to meet the foe, and, of course, the young armor-bearer went in the king's train. A fierce battle ensued. Soon, the combatants were all so smeared with blood and dust that no man could tell friend from foe. The young armor-bearer was in the thick of the fray and, thinking himself among the enemy, laid blow upon blow on any man who came near him. Unfortunately, one of his blows landed upon his sovereign, severing his arm from his body.

"The king recognized his armor-bearer as the one who had dealt him the blow, and with many imprecations against him, quit the field, for his injury was so severe there was no way he could continue the fight. When the Persian army saw their king withdraw from the battle grievously wounded, they fell into disarray, and the field was lost. The king sued for peace, and a truce was reached with the enemy ruler upon payment of an extortionate sum of money. The armor-bearer was clapped in irons and thrown into prison, with none of his protestations of innocence given any heed.

"The king was taken on a litter back to his apartments, where he was tended by the best physicians in the land, both day and night. However, all their efforts were in vain. The wound festered, and soon it became apparent that the king had not much longer to live. The king, therefore, summoned the vizier who had foretold his death and said to him, 'You prophesied that I would be killed by my own son when he reached his twentieth year, but you see that I have not. I have been mortally wounded by my armor-bearer, the son of one of the palace secretaries. Your life, therefore, is forfeit, for your prophecy was false.'

"The vizier replied, 'It may be as your illustrious majesty says, but first we should have the armor-bearer brought here so that we might ask him about his origins. Your majesty doubtless would not want to execute an innocent man.'

"The king agreed that this course was just, and so the armor-bearer was taken from prison and brought before the king and the vizier. 'Tell me,' said the king to the young man, 'where are you from and who are your parents?'

"'I know not the country of my origin and I know not my parents, save that I was told that my father was a king. When I was but an infant, my nurse and I were lodged in an underground chamber. When I attained the age of seven years, a lion forced his way into our dwelling, where he savaged and devoured my nurse and then carried me up to the top of a mountain. There the lion loosed his grip, and I tumbled down to the foot of the mountain. That is where the secretary found me. He took me into his home and raised me as his own son until your majesty took me into your service.'

"The King of Persia then recognized the armor-bearer as his own son, and so handed to him his throne, and made the vizier the prime minister of the land. Three days later, the king died from his wounds."

Having concluded his tale, Bakhtiyar said to King Azadbakht, "This is why, O glorious king, I said that I was like the King of Persia, for though I might struggle against the dictates of Heaven, I must go to the fate that awaits me, whether I will it or not."

The Fate of Bakhtiyar

Azadbakht was moved by the young man's story and ordered the guards to take him back to his prison cell. Upon hearing this, the viziers all stood up and protested, saying they would resign their posts and leave the country if the execution was not held forthwith.

"Very well. The execution may go forward. But I, for one, will not witness it—my heart could not bear to see this young man put to death. You must take him and do the deed yourselves," said Azadbakht.

The viziers then proclaimed that Bakhtiyar was to be executed in the public square at midday. They had the gallows prepared in the main square and ordered the people to witness the event.

Now, it happened that Firokh Suvar, Bakhtiyar's foster father, had come to the city with some of his companions on business of his own that day, and he was wearing the golden cloak in which he had found the infant at the side of the well. Firokh saw the crowds assembling and the gallows prepared. He did not wish to watch the execution, so he began to resume his journey to where he intended to do business. Just then, the crowd parted to let the guards come through with the prisoner, and Firokh recognized his dear son weighed down with many chains.

Firokh and his friends rushed to the young man's aid, and after wresting him away from the guards, Firokh made loud demands to have an audience with the king.

When he was brought before Azadbakht, Firokh said, "I beg of your most illustrious majesty not to kill this young man! This is my beloved son, a man of good heart, and I know that he must be innocent of any crime of which he has been accused. If you must have blood, take mine as well, for I cannot live without him."

"Your wish certainly can be granted," said Azadbakht.

"O my king, you know not what foolishness this is! Surely this youth is the son of a mighty king and queen. Think of what they would do if they found that you had killed their child!"

"First, you protested that he is your son, but now you say he is someone else's. Tell the truth, or I really shall have you executed along with him."

"I am telling the truth, O my king and O the delight of the world. I found my son at the edge of a well in the desert, an infant wrapped in the very cloak I am wearing now. And around his neck was a bracelet of ten pearls, which I carry with me to this day."

Firokh took out the bracelet of pearls and showed them to Azadbakht, who recognized them and the cloak as the things he and his queen had left with their infant son when they had abandoned him in the wilderness. He then asked Firokh to give him the cloak and the pearls, whereupon he took them to the queen and showed them to her.

"Why these are the cloak and pearls we left with our dear son! How did you come upon them? Does our son yet live? Tell me!" she said.

"I shall do better than tell you. I shall bring him here in the flesh."

The king then sent servants to fetch Bakhtiyar. When Bakhtiyar arrived, Azadbakht struck off his chains and put a royal turban on his head. Then he wrapped the young man in a royal cloak and conducted him to the queen.

"This is our son, O my wife, who we left at the well," said Azadbakht.

When the queen heard this, milk sprang from her breasts.

The king and the queen embraced Bakhtiyar with great joy and many tears of happiness.

Then the king said to the queen, "Tell me, why did you propose to destroy this young man with false testimony?"

"Your viziers came to me and told me that your anger against me would be boundless were I not to confess what they told me to confess. I resisted as long as I could, but in the end, I had to give in to them," said the queen.

At this, Azadbakht fell into a rage. He ordered the immediate execution of all ten viziers, who died that very day on the gallows they had prepared for Bakhtiyar. Azadbakht then turned over his kingdom to Bakhtiyar, who made Firokh Suvar his chief vizier and gave positions of authority to Firokh's companions. The people all rejoiced that Azadbakht and his queen had been reunited with their son, and they pledged their fidelity and love for their new ruler. Bakhtiyar had a long and prosperous reign, and ever did he rule over his people with wisdom and justice.

Section III: Tales from the Shahnameh

The Tale of Kayumars and Hushang

The first few stories in the Shahnameh *are tales of ancient and likely mythical kings. The one retold below is set in a mythical past when human beings could still communicate directly with animals, birds, and supernatural creatures such as fairies. As is common with such stories, the earliest kings are credited with discovering or inventing things that are basic to human survival, such as clothing and fire. Here we learn of the discovery of fire and of the origin of the festival of Sadeh, which still takes place every year today, fifty days before No-Ruz, the Iranian New Year, which is celebrated on the vernal equinox. As a midwinter festival, Sadeh celebrates fire's ability to defeat the cold and looks forward to the spring that is yet to come.*

The very first king of Persia was a man named Kayumars. He wore clothing made of leopard skins, and so did his people, for other forms of clothing had not yet been made. It was Kayumars who first learned how to make clothing and prepare food, and he taught these things to the people. Kayumars was tall and strong, and the glory of his power shone out from him so that all bowed down before his presence, even the animals, both wild and tame.

Kayumars had one son, whose name was Siamak. Siamak was fair of face and very wise. Kayumars loved Siamak more than anything else in the world, and Siamak was the source of all Kayumars's joy.

Now, Siamak had no enemies among the people, for he was wise and just. However, Ahriman looked upon him and greatly envied him, and so vowed to destroy him. Ahriman went to his own son, a demon who hungered for destruction as a wolf hungered for prey, and told him to gather an army and attack Kayumars's kingdom so that it might be destroyed, and to kill Siamak.

Ahriman made his plans in secret, so Kayumars knew nothing of the danger he was in. But the angel Sorush appeared to Siamak in a dream, warning him of the approaching army. Siamak was enraged by this and mustered an army of his own. Siamak and his soldiers went to war clad only in leopard skins, for armor was yet to be invented. When Siamak and his army arrived at the place where Ahriman's son had arrayed his own soldiers, Siamak rushed forward to attack Ahriman's demon son. The battle did not last long; the demon took his long, sharp claws and drove them into Siamak's body, killing him.

When Kayumars heard that Siamak was dead, he fell into deep grief. He wept and tore at his beard, and all his kingdom wept with him, for Siamak had been much loved. The army arrayed itself before Kayumars and sent up a shout of grief. All the people dressed in blue to show that they, too, mourned Siamak. Even the animals and birds grieved for the death of that noble young man.

The entire kingdom mourned for one year, and then one night, Sorush appeared to Kayumars in a dream.

Sorush said, "Grieve no more. The time of your vengeance is near. If you muster your army and march out against the demon, you will have your revenge."

Now, Siamak himself had a son, a noble young man named Hushang. No one could match Hushang for intelligence or courtliness, and Kayumars relied on Hushang's good counsel and bravery.

Kayumars said to Hushang, "The time of our vengeance has come. Muster an army and lead it forth. I would lead it myself, but I am an old man now, so that duty must fall to you."

Hushang did as his grandfather bid him. He assembled a great army of fairies and all manner of savage beasts, and birds, cattle, and sheep. The army rode out with Hushang in the lead and Kayumars in the rear. Soon they met the army of demons, and a fierce battle took place. This time the demons were no match for Hushang's army. The lions, tigers, and other fierce beasts tore the demon soldiers to shreds, and Siamak himself met the demon who had killed his father and clove him in two. Then, he cut the demon's head off and flayed the skin off his body.

Having avenged his son, Kayumars died, and Hushang took over the throne. Hushang ruled justly and wisely, and his kingdom prospered under his rule.

One day, Hushang rode into the mountains with some companions. Suddenly a great black dragon appeared before them. It had blood-red eyes, and smoke and flame issued from its gaping mouth. Hushang picked up a rock and flung it at the beast. The beast dodged the rock and then went away, but this was not the end of the adventure; when the rock struck the stones that stood behind the dragon, a great shower of sparks went up. This is how Hushang discovered that flint might be used to make fire and how the people first learned to make and use fire. Hushang deemed this a great gift from God, and from that day forth, the people always prayed to God facing a fire.

That night, Hushang and his friends made a great bonfire and held a feast. They danced around the fire, celebrating and drinking wine, and this is how the feast of Sadeh came to be.

Now that Hushang knew how to make fire, he then set out to see what other things might come from the rocks around him. He took some ore and smelted it, and in this way, he discovered iron. Then he took the iron and made many useful things, such as hatchets, maces, and saws. Next, Hushang looked for a way to bring more water into his kingdom. He dug channels to bring water into the fields and thus invented irrigation. Once the people had a good source of water, they could plant more crops and grow more grain and fruit, and thus Hushang's kingdom prospered greatly.

Hushang also decreed which animals were to be domesticated and which were to remain wild. He decreed which animals could be hunted and which were to serve the people. He learned how to catch and flay fur-bearing animals like squirrels and ermine and turn their pelts into warm clothing.

Hushang worked tirelessly to better his kingdom and make it more prosperous. He dispensed justice and ruled with wisdom. However, for all his wisdom, Hushang was still a mortal man, and at the end of his days, he perished, as must we all.

Jamshid the Magnificent

Kayumars and Hushang may have benefited humanity through their discoveries of fire, metalworking, and clothing, but their accomplishments pale compared to those of Jamshid. Jamshid builds on discovering metalworking by inventing armor for both men and horses, discovering how to spin and weave fibers into thread and cloth and how to dye those materials, and create a social order within his kingdom.

Unfortunately, Jamshid falls victim to the sin of pride, thinking that his success as king makes his glory rival even that of God. Jamshid learns a hard lesson about this when his kingdom is captured by Zahhak, a neighboring prince who has been corrupted by Iblis. In the character of Iblis, the Muslim devil, we see Islam as part of the Persian culture that Ferdowsi knew, even though the story is set in a time before the advent of Islam.

The Reign of Jamshid

Jamshid was the son of King Tahmures and was determined to be a good king like his father, and indeed the whole world submitted to Jamshid's royal power. Not only did the people acknowledge him as king, but so did the birds and animals, and even the demons and fairies bowed before him.

Of himself, Jamshid said, "I am king, and I am priest. The grace of God is mine, and it shines forth from me. I will put down the evil-doers, and the soul of the people I will guide toward the light."

The first thing Jamshid did upon assuming the throne was turn his thought to his army and what sorts of weapons and armor they ought to have. Jamshid invented helmets and chain mail, breastplates and swords. Jamshid did not neglect his soldiers' mounts—he even invented armor for the horses to wear. For fifty years, Jamshid worked at equipping his army, and when the fifty years were over, he had a great store of weapons and armor, greater than any other in the world.

In the next fifty years of his reign, Jamshid turned his mind to the making of thread and cloth. He invented spinning and weaving and taught the people how to take wool, flax, and silk and turn them into thread and cloth. Then, he taught the people how to cut and sew the cloth into clothing and dye the cloth to wear bright colors. The people all rejoiced in this, and so did Jamshid.

For the third fifty years, Jamshid considered how best to order the people themselves. He did this by dividing them into castes and giving each caste its place within the kingdom. The first caste was of people who spent their days in prayer and worship. Jamshid sent these to live in the mountains. The second caste was that of the warriors, the men who were skilled in battle and whose loyalty and courage supported the king's rule. The third caste was those who worked the fields and grew the crops that all might eat. These people were free and not slaves—although they had much hard labor. The fourth caste was the artisans and craftsmen, people who made good things with their hands. It took Jamshid fifty years to divide the people in this way and teach them how they must live and do their duties.

When that work was complete, Jamshid turned his mind to the creation of buildings. He told the demons under his command to take clay, use it to make bricks, and then take the bricks and use them along with stone and wood to create baths and palaces. Jamshid also opened mines so that he might have precious gems. He used magic for this and the mining of precious ores, such as silver and gold.

Jamshid discovered perfumes and taught the people how to use ambergris, sandalwood, rosewater, and many other things to create lovely scents. He also studied what things were good for medicine, and in this way, showed people how to cure illnesses and live healthy lives.

Next, Jamshid discovered how to build ships and sail them across the water. He spent another fifty years in this labor, which allowed him to travel very quickly from one place to another.

Now, Jamshid had accomplished more than any king, living or dead, but still, he was not satisfied. He built himself a golden throne, all studded with hundreds of gems.

When the throne was built, he said to the demons that served him, "Raise me up into the heavens so that my glory might shine like the sun."

Jamshid did this on the first day of the month of Farvardin, and he called that day No-Ruz, or New Day, and said that from thenceforth, it would be the first day of the year. The nobles of Jamshid's court rejoiced in this and made a great feast to celebrate, and indeed, even today, the people celebrate No-Ruz in memory of Jamshid.

For three hundred years, Jamshid's people prospered under his rule. In those days, death was unknown, the demons served the people, and the people served their king. For three hundred years, Jamshid's royal glory shone down upon his people.

Jamshid looked upon them and thought, *The whole world is mine to command. My light shines down upon the people and makes them prosperous. Who is like me? Who is more powerful than I?*

Jamshid had forgotten that he was still a man, after all, and not God.

Jamshid then summoned all his counselors and generals and wise men.

He said to them, "Who is like me? Who else rules the whole world? It was I who taught the people how to live, how to weave and sew, how to build. Every good thing that you have comes from me and my works. Surely there is no king in all the Earth but me."

The counselors, generals, and wise men all bowed their heads in assent—although they knew what Jamshid said was folly; they were too frightened of what the king might do to speak the truth to him.

But God was not afraid of Jamshid. God heard what Jamshid said and how Jamshid tried to outdo God in glory and power. On that day, God removed his glory from Jamshid. No longer did Jamshid shine upon his people as the Sun shone upon the Earth, and no longer were the people loyal to him. Some began to whisper against him, and sedition spread across the land, but it was the Arab prince Zahhak who caused Jamshid's final downfall, and now we must learn how that came about.

Zahhak the Demon Prince

In the time of Jamshid, the king of the Arabs was a kind and generous man named Merdas. He did his best to rule wisely and well. His herds numbered in the thousands, and no one who needed milk ever went without it.

Merdas had a son named Zahhak, who was as ambitious and grasping as his father was just and generous. Zahhak had an evil temper, and all who knew him understood that they had best stay out of his way. Just as Merdas had great herds of sheep and cattle that he used to feed the people, Zahhak had a great herd of horses with golden bridles for each one, and Zahhak rode everywhere to show how great and powerful he was.

One morning, a man walked up to Zahhak and said, "Greetings, O prince. I trust that you are well?"

"Yes, I am well. State your business," said Zahhak.

Now, what Zahhak did not know was that this was no ordinary man. No, it was Iblis himself, come to make a bargain.

Iblis said, "I'll tell you my business, but only if you promise not to tell anyone else what we talked about today."

"Certainly. I will keep our conversation secret."

"Good. This is why I have come to you: To give you my advice. I've seen you riding up and down on your horses with golden bridles. You're obviously a very powerful man. You could do a lot of good things if the throne were yours. Your father is old—he can't have many years left anyway, so take the throne from him. You'll be a better king than him."

"Wait, I can't do that! Yes, I do want to be king, but I'll not kill my father for it."

"You have to. If you don't do what I tell you to, you'll be breaking your promise to me. Your father will stay on the throne forever, and you'll never be anything other than a very highly placed subject."

At this, Zahhak relented. "Tell me what I have to do."

"Don't worry about it. I'll take care of everything."

Now, one of King Merdas's habits was to go into the orchard that grew near the palace each morning before sunrise. There, he would bathe and say his prayers. Both the king and the servant who accompanied him knew the way by heart, so neither had a lamp. Iblis knew this, so he went into the orchard at night and dug a deep pit along the path Merdas would be taking. When Merdas went to the orchard that morning, he fell into the pit and broke his back. Merdas died from his injuries, and as soon as Iblis saw that the king's life had departed him, he filled the pit back in with soil and left.

Zahhak soon learned of his father's misfortune. Zahhak took the throne of the Arabs and put the crown upon his head. Iblis was delighted to see that Zahhak was now on the throne.

He went to Zahhak and said, "I have some more advice for you. Do whatever I tell you, and you will have anything you could ever desire. You will be the most powerful man in the whole world."

Then, Iblis left Zahhak's court.

After a time, Iblis came back, again having disguised himself as a young man.

He went before Zahhak and said, "If it pleases your majesty, I am a very good cook and at your service."

Zahhak liked the look of the young cook, and so employed him on the spot. He gave Iblis the key to the kitchen and larders and put him in charge of preparing all the meals. In those days, people did not eat much meat, but most of the dishes that Iblis prepared for the king were made of birds' or animals' flesh. In this way, Iblis hoped to make Zahhak follow his orders, and since lions also live on the flesh of other animals, Iblis intended to make Zahhak as brave as a lion by feeding him flesh.

However, first Iblis made a dish of egg yolks for the king.

"This is a very good dish. Everyone who has ever eaten this becomes very healthy," Iblis said.

The king ate the egg yolks and found them to be delicious.

"That was a very good meal," he said and rewarded the cook.

"That was just the beginning, your majesty. Wait until you see what I will prepare tomorrow!"

The next day, Iblis prepared a dish of partridge and pheasant.

On the third day, he made a dish of chicken and lamb. Zahhak was delighted by each of these and rewarded the cook well.

On the fourth day, Iblis prepared a dish of veal cooked in wine and rosewater and seasoned with many spices. He brought it to Zahhak, and when the king had tasted it, he could not believe how good it was.

"Truly, I have never tasted anything so splendid. Whatever you want from me, you shall have it. Just name it, and it is yours," said the king.

"I am grateful to your majesty. May you live forever. Truly, your glory shall shine throughout the Earth. I have but one humble request: Allow me to kiss your shoulders."

Zahhak thought this an odd request, but he had already promised to give the cook whatever he asked, so he said, "Certainly, you may kiss my shoulders."

Iblis went up to Zahhak and kissed the king's shoulders. No sooner had Iblis finished the second kiss than he disappeared. Zahhak blinked in astonishment, but he had no time to consider that strange occurrence because something was happening to his shoulders in the places where the cook had kissed him. Zahhak looked and was appalled to see that one black snake was growing out of each shoulder. Zahhak tried everything he could think of to make the snakes go away, but nothing worked, not even cutting them off, because no matter how many times he cut them off, they would instantly grow back. Zahhak consulted every doctor he could find. He summoned doctors from faraway lands. But none of the doctors, no matter how learned, could give him a remedy.

Finally, a new doctor appeared at Zahhak's court. It was none other than Iblis, who had disguised himself yet again.

"I know these snakes distress you greatly, but I think it is your fate to bear them. The best thing you can do is feed them. They'll eat fresh meat, and that will pacify them. If you feed them human brains, though, that might kill them." Iblis said this because he was hoping that Zahhak would kill all the people to get rid of the snakes.

In this way, Iblis's desire to destroy humanity would come to pass.

The Downfall of Jamshid

Now, while Iblis was tempting Zahhak in the land of the Arabs, Jamshid was having difficulties in Persia. His royal glory no longer shone upon the land, and where he had once ruled wisely and well, he now had become ungenerous and unjust. Many of the nobles decided that they would make better kings than Jamshid, so they marshaled their own armies and staked out their own territories, saying that they had claims to the throne and would take it by force if necessary.

Some Persian nobles came to hear about the snake-shouldered king of the Arabs.

"There's a king who could help us. He'll get rid of Jamshid for sure," they said.

So, they sent an embassy to the court of Zahhak to see whether he would aid them in their quest to unseat Jamshid.

When they came before Zahhak, the ambassadors said, "O great one, surely there is no king like yourself. You rule all of Arabia, but surely your realm should be greater than that. Surely the throne of Persia also should be yours."

Zahhak listened to their flattery and decided to help them. He gathered his army and went to the aid of the Persian nobles. By this time, Jamshid had few supporters, and so his warriors could not withstand the onslaught. Jamshid was put to flight, and Zahhak put the crown of Persia upon his head.

For one hundred years, Jamshid hid from Zahhak, but Zahhak never stopped seeking him.

One day, word came to Zahhak that Jamshid had been spied near the Sea of China. Zahhak sent his soldiers to capture Jamshid. They brought Jamshid before Zahhak, and although Jamshid begged for mercy, Zahhak simply had him sawn in two.

Jamshid lived for seven hundred years, and in that time, he did many good things and many evil things. However, what good does long life do to anyone—since the world never reveals all its secrets but instead waits until we are unwary and then sends us an evil fate?

The Birth of Zal

Zal is one of the great heroes of the Shahnameh, *eclipsed only by his mighty son, Rostam. That Zal is destined for great and unusual things is signaled by the fact that he is born with white hair—a feature that seems to have been associated with demonic origins. (We will see this later in the description of the White Demon faced by Rostam.)*

Zal's father initially abandons his child, who is rescued and reared by the fearsome but kindly Simorgh, whose nurture turns the already extraordinary Zal into a great hero. The Simorgh is an animal from Persian myth with the body of a bird and the head of a lion. The Simorgh is always female, but sometimes she also has a peacock's tail. In ancient Iranian culture, the Simorgh was associated with both fertility and kingship.

Once there was a mighty warrior named Sam, who served at the court of King Manuchehr. Sam was strong, brave, and loyal, and won every battle he fought. However, he also was very sad because he had no child. He prayed many times for God to ease his sadness, and finally, those prayers were answered. One of his wives found herself with child, and when her time came, she delivered a strong, healthy boy. The baby was well made in all his limbs, and his face was the most beautiful anyone had ever seen, with lovely dark eyes. There was but one strange thing about this child: His hair was as white as snow.

The women of Sam's household were frightened to tell Sam about his child because they feared he would become angry if he knew the baby had white hair like that of an old man.

After a week had passed, the boy's wet nurse gathered all her courage and went to tell Sam about the birth of his son.

"May it please your honor, and may you live forever in great prosperity, with all your enemies under your feet, a boy child has been born to you," she said.

"Praise be to God! Finally, my desire has been fulfilled. Come, tell me about the boy. Is he healthy? Is he beautiful? How does he fare?" said Sam.

"Your son is as beautiful as a summer's day. He is well made in all his limbs. His face is as beautiful and radiant as the sun, and he has lovely dark eyes."

"Ah, that is well to hear. Tell me more."

"As I said, your honor, the boy is healthy and beautiful. There is but one thing about him that you might think ill . . . he has hair as white as snow."

Upon hearing this, Sam went immediately to the women's quarters to see his son. The boy was indeed all that the nurse had said he was: Beautiful, radiant, and strong. But all of this was marred in Sam's eyes by the boy's thatch of pure white hair.

"What have I done to deserve this? What sin have I committed that my son is cursed to look like an old man on the day of his birth? People will think that he is a demon's child, and I will never be able to show my face for shame," Sam cried.

Sam then ordered his men to take the child, now named Zal for his white hair, up into the mountains. "Expose him on the hillside. If anyone wishes to raise that wretched creature, let them take him. I want nothing more to do with him."

Thus, the child Zal was taken up into the mountains and left upon the hillside, all alone.

Now, those mountains were the home of the Simorgh, and it was there that she had her nest and raised her chicks. No sooner had Sam's men left the baby Zal on the hillside than the Simorgh flew out to find meat to feed her young. The Simorgh flew to and fro, looking for an animal or a bird that would make a good meal for her chicks. Suddenly, she heard the squall of an infant. She descended to the place the sound was coming from, and there she saw the baby, laid naked on the rock, with no one to tend him.

I wonder who left this child here, the Simorgh thought. *But no matter. Where he comes from isn't important if he'll feed my chicks.*

The Simorgh took the baby in her claws and flew back to her nest. When she arrived, she placed the baby in the nest, thinking that her chicks would feast on his flesh, but instead, something strange and wonderful happened. When the Simorgh and her young looked upon the boy and heard his cries, they pitied him and did not devour him.

The Simorgh went hunting again, this time bringing back a goat. She fed part of the goat to her young and then held up some of its flesh for the baby to suckle. In this way, the Simorgh raised Zal as though he were her own, and in time, he grew into a strong young man with mighty shoulders and a broad chest. Caravans passing near the Simorgh's dwelling sometimes caught sight of the lad, and soon tales of him began to be told throughout Persia.

Now, Sam soon heard tell of this wondrous youth with white hair, but he paid the tales no mind until one night he had a dream. In the dream, a man from India rode toward him on an Arabian horse.

The man said, "My lord, I bring you tidings of your son, Zal. He lives in the mountains, in the nest of the Simorgh. He is as strong as an ox and as brave as a lion, and his beauty is radiant like the sun."

When the man had delivered his message, Sam woke up.

Sam did not know how to understand his dream. He summoned his priests and other wise men.

He told them his dream and said, "You are the wisest men in all Persia. What do you think this means?"

The priests and wise men replied, "All creatures of the world love their young and rear them with kindness. Even the most vicious leopard takes care of her cubs. But you have treated your son most evilly. You cast him out when he was but an infant, leaving him to die on the mountainside. You should pray to God for forgiveness, for your sin has been great."

Sam's heart was troubled by these words, and when night fell, he had another dream. He dreamed he was in India, at the foot of a mountain. Before him was a great army, led by a beautiful slave. On one side of the slave was a wise sage, and on the other, a priest.

One of these came forward and said to Sam, "You have greatly sinned before God. You prayed for a son, yet when God granted your wish, you cast your son out into the wilderness. Why should white hair trouble you so? After all, your hair and beard are white as snow, yet you count yourself a good man. It is fortunate that God's love is greater than your shame and that he sent the Simorgh to look after your child—the child you asked for and then despised."

At this, Sam cried out in his sleep.

In the morning, Sam summoned his chief advisers and the leaders of his army and set out for the mountains where the Simorgh lived. Sam traveled through the mountains until he finally came to the highest and sheerest of all the peaks, and on the very top was the nest of the Simorgh. The nest was made from ebony and sandalwood woven together and looked like a great palace.

When Sam saw the Simorgh's nest, he fell to his knees and bowed his face to the ground.

Not lifting his eyes, he prayed, "O God who made all things, I give thanks to you for the great Simorgh, the mightiest of all your creatures. You who are the most just and the most powerful, hear my prayer. If the youth who lives with the Simorgh is indeed my son and not the child of a demon, help me find my way to him."

As Sam was kneeling and making his prayer, the Simorgh spied him there at the foot of the mountain, and she knew the time had come for her human son to return to his people.

The Simorgh said to the young man, "You have grown up in my nest and are like one of my own chicks. But now your human father waits at the foot of the mountain, and I must return you to him."

"I do not want to leave. This is my home. Have I been a burden? Is that why you wish to dispose of me?" said Zal.

The Simorgh replied, "This nest may have been your home, but fate has an even more glorious home in store for you. Your father is none other than the hero Sam, who lives in a palace far more beautiful than my nest. Here, take two of my feathers. If ever you need me, place a feather in the fire and summon me. I will take the form of a black cloud and come to fetch you back here."

Then the Simorgh gently took the youth in her claws and flew down to where his father was waiting. Her heart was very heavy, for she did not want to part with the young man whom she had raised as her own. The Simorgh set Zal down gently in front of Sam, who bowed low before the great bird and did her much honor.

When Sam looked at his son, he wept tears of joy, for Zal was even more beautiful than the tales had said. He was tall and strong, with a mighty chest and mighty limbs, and his white hair flowed over his shoulders down to the middle of his body. Sam threw a cloak over his son's body and led him down the mountainside, where the youth was dressed in clothing befitting a king. Then Sam mounted Zal on the finest of his horses.

When the army saw Sam's son, they cheered and rejoiced, for none of them had ever seen a youth as beautiful or as strong, and they were glad that he was reunited with his father. Sam ordered that drummers be mounted on elephants and lead the army, playing all the way home.

At the gates of the city, all manner of musicians awaited Sam's return. As soon as they saw his army approaching, they let up a great din of trumpets, cymbals, and drums to celebrate Sam's homecoming with his son Zal, and all the city set to feasting in celebration.

The Seven Trials of Rostam

Rostam is perhaps the greatest hero in ancient Persian myth. The son of Zal, whom we met in the previous story, has all the qualities one would expect of such a champion. Rostam is supernaturally strong and skilled with weaponry, and he is so tall and heavy, even as a very young man, that no ordinary horse can bear his weight. A significant number of the tales in the Shahnameh *are dedicated to the exploits of Rostam.*

Rostam's closest companion is Rakhsh, a stallion who can understand human speech. Like Rostam, Rakhsh has supernatural qualities. He is a chestnut roan, but instead of the usual white hairs mixed in with the chestnut, Rakhsh has golden hairs. Of all the horses in Persia, only Rakhsh is big and strong enough to carry both Rostam and his weapons, one of which is a giant mace.

"The Seven Trials of Rostam" relates the deeds of Rostam as he rides out to rescue the Persian King Kavus and his army after they have fallen into the clutches of an evil demon during a campaign to destroy Mazandaran, a country under the sway of evil beings. It is Rostam's father, Zal, who orders him to effect this rescue, telling him that this deed is the reason why Rostam was born and what he was meant to do. Rostam readily agrees and promises not to return unless he is victorious.

(Note on terminology: In this story, distances are given in ancient Persian units called parasangs. *One parasang was the distance a man could walk in an hour, and is equivalent to about six kilometers or about three miles.)*

The First Trial: The Lion

When Rostam heard that King Kavus and his army were in the clutches of an evil demon, he took up his weapons, saddled his horse, and set out on the road that would bring him to Mazandaran. Rostam rode all day and into the night, and when dawn came, he found himself to be tired and hungry.

He rode on until he came to a plain where a herd of wild asses was grazing. Rostam took out his lariat and urged Rakhsh into a gallop. Rostam and Rakhsh chased down one of the asses, and soon Rostam had captured one and killed it. Rostam then built a fire and skinned the ass, and when all was ready, he roasted the meat and ate it straight off the bone. However, Rostam did not only think about his hunger; he removed Rakhsh's bridle and turned him loose to graze on the good grass that grew in that place.

His hunger sated, Rostam went to the nearby river, where he cut enough reeds to make himself a comfortable bed. He lay down by the fire and fell asleep, while Rakhsh stood guard over him.

Now, Rostam and Rakhsh were unaware that behind the reed bed was the den of a lion. The lion had been out hunting when Rostam arrived, but he came home soon after Rostam went to sleep. The lion looked at the giant of a warrior who lay on a bed of reeds, and then he looked at the warrior's horse. Calculating that it would be wise to kill the horse first, the lion pounced at Rakhsh. The lion was no match for the horse. Rakhsh met the lion's assault with his hooves, splitting the lion's skull asunder. Then Rakhsh sank his teeth into the lion's back and tossed the animal onto the ground, where Rakhsh proceeded to trample it with his hooves until the lion was quite dismembered.

Rostam awoke during the night and saw what remained of the lion.

He said to Rakhsh, "Why did you deal with that lion all by yourself? That wasn't a very smart thing to do, not when I was here to help you. What would I have done if the lion had killed you? I can't very well walk all the way to Mazandaran. Next time, wake me up. Don't fight by yourself."

The Second Trial: The Spring of Water

In the morning, Rostam said his prayers, and then gave Rakhsh a rubdown and put on his saddle. Rostam took up his weapons and mounted the horse. He urged Rakhsh forward, and so they began the next portion of their journey.

Their way forward led across a desert, and after many miles, both Rostam and Rakhsh were beset by thirst. Rakhsh was stumbling with weariness and panting, while Rostam was weak in his body, and his lips were parched and cracked. Rostam dismounted and led Rakhsh by the reins.

Rostam turned his eyes to Heaven and said, "Almighty God, I pray you for mercy. You know that my task is to rescue King Kavus from the demons and that I do this because you command it. Have mercy upon us all, we who walk this earth and are tormented by thirst."

No sooner had he finished his prayer than the mighty Rostam fell to the dusty earth, unable to take even one more step forward. Just then, a fat ram ran across the path, and Rostam's spirits rose.

"Come, Rakhsh. Let's follow that ram. It's so sleek and fat—there must be water nearby. God surely has sent the ram as a sign of his mercy and compassion," he said.

Rostam and Rakhsh followed the ram, which soon led them to a freshwater stream that flowed along merrily.

Rostam said, "Surely the one true God is the only God, and blessed are those who trust in him!" Then he cried after the ram, "Blessings upon you, friend! May you always have the best of grass and the clearest of water, and may no beast take you as its prey! May no hunter's arrows ever strike you! If not for you, my horse and I would surely be carrion for the vultures!"

Rostam unsaddled Rakhsh, and both of them drank deeply. Rostam took off all his clothing and bathed in the clear, cool water, and when he was thus refreshed, he found that he was hungry. Therefore, he took his bow and arrows and went in search of something to eat. He came upon a wild ass, which he brought down with an arrow and then skinned. He roasted the meat over an open fire and ate the meat straight off the bone. When his meal was done, he went back to the stream and drank deeply of the fresh water.

Satisfied body and soul, Rostam lay down near the fire and said to Rakhsh, "Remember what I said: No fighting by yourself. Wake me if any demons or dangerous beasts come here."

Then Rostam went to sleep, and Rakhsh grazed nearby, keeping watch over his friend.

The Third Trial: The Dragon

Rakhsh grazed peacefully until midnight when, in the distance, he spied a huge dragon heading toward him and Rostam. He nudged Rostam awake, but when Rostam arose, the dragon hid in the shadows so that Rostam saw nothing.

"Jumping at shadows, old friend?" said Rostam, who was annoyed at having been awoken. "Don't wake me up unless there's something really there."

Then Rostam lay down and went back to sleep.

As soon as the dragon saw that Rostam had returned to his rest, he again started slithering toward the hero's camp. Again, Rakhsh woke Rostam, and again, the dragon hid so that Rostam saw nothing. Rostam was very angry this time.

"What is wrong with you? I swear, if you wake me up again and I see there's nothing there, I'll cut off your feet and walk all the way to Mazandaran," said Rostam.

He lay down a third time and went back to sleep, and a third time, the dragon resumed its path toward the hero. Smoke and flames billowed from its mouth, but Rakhsh dared not wake Rostam a third time. Rakhsh bolted away from the monster, but then his love for Rostam brought him galloping back. This time, instead of waking Rostam gently, Rakhsh neighed and stamped at the ground. Rostam awoke, utterly furious, but this time, the dragon did not hide quickly enough, and Rostam saw it.

Rostam drew his sword and said to the dragon, "Tell me your name. I don't like killing my enemies without knowing who they are, and I intend to kill you."

The dragon replied, "I am he who rules in this place. My claws are sharper than spear points, and neither man nor beast dares tread upon this land. Even eagles fear to fly above it, and the stars fear to shine. Now tell me your name because your mother will soon weep for you."

"I am Rostam, son of Zal, son of Sam, of the line of Nariman," said Rostam, and at that, the dragon leaped at him, and a battle ensued.

Rostam fought well, but soon the dragon used its weight against him, and Rostam faltered. When Rakhsh saw this, he raced in to help his friend, barreling into the dragon with his own body and knocking the great, snaky beast back. Then Rakhsh attacked with hooves and teeth, and even Rostam wondered at the horse's ferocity.

Finally, Rostam saw his chance. He slashed with his sword, cutting the monster's head clean off its body. Poisonous blood gushed out of the wound, seeping into the desert floor and dissolving the very soil. Rostam had never seen so much blood and had never known a poison so deadly, and he was afraid. He went into a nearby stream and bathed his body and clothing, praying all the while.

When his prayer and bath alike were done, Rostam mounted his horse and resumed his journey.

The Fourth Trial: The Witch

Rostam rode through what was left of the night and into the next day. When the sun had begun to set, he arrived at a fair country shaded by many trees, through which a river of clear water was running. Near the river, a meal had been set out, with roasted fowl heaped high on platters, and bowls mounded full of rice mixed with dates and spices, and fresh cucumbers and candied fruits, and goblets of wine, and fine cushions for the guests to sit on. This was a feast set out for the sorcerers who lived in that land, but the sorcerers had run away and hid when they heard Rakhsh's hoofbeats approaching.

Rostam dismounted and unsaddled Rakhsh when he saw the feast spread before him, with no one there to enjoy it. He then sat down in front of the food and noticed a lute among the cushions, platters, and plates. Rostam picked up the lute and began to play it. To amuse himself, he made up a song to go along with the melody he played.

Rostam am I, hero brave and bold,
My days are numbered, I won't live to be old.
A paladin, I travel to where the battles are,
I have no feather bed, I sleep under the stars.
Demons, dragons, warriors all
Beneath the might of my sword do fall.
Across deserts bright and mountains high
I journey on and on, and rarely do I
Find a resting place of peace and plenty,
With wine and song and friends about me.
No, to fight with demons is my fate,

For that's the hero's true estate.

Now, among the sorcerers was a witch, and when she heard Rostam's song, she decided to see what manner of man he was. She disguised herself as a beautiful young woman dressed in the finest of silks, with flowing black hair and lovely dark eyes.

She sat down next to Rostam and said, "Greetings, stranger. Please, partake of the food and wine, but as you do so, tell me who you are and where you are from."

When the woman sat down, Rostam could scarcely believe his luck, and he praised God in his heart for sending him not only such good food and drink but also a beautiful woman to share it with.

Rostam handed the woman a goblet of wine and said, "I am Rostam and have traveled very far. Give thanks to God with me that this feast is here and that we may enjoy it together."

At the mention of God's name, the witch's face blurred and twisted.

Rostam quickly took his lariat and ensnared the witch's head with it, and when he had her well tied up, Rostam said, "Tell me who you really are. Show me your true self."

The young woman's face and body changed until a withered old hag stood before Rostam. She cursed both God and Rostam, and at this, Rostam knew her to be a witch.

He took his dagger and cut her in two, and when the other sorcerers saw this, they were frightened and remained in hiding.

The Fifth Trial: The Capture of Olad

Rostam left the sorcerers' land behind him and rode until he came to a country where all was black as night. Neither the Sun nor Moon nor stars were visible. Rostam picked his way forward as carefully as he could, not knowing what the road underfoot would prove to be like, nor what might be coming toward him and his valiant horse in the pitch blackness. For all its horrors, the dark country proved to be a relatively small place, and soon Rostam and Rakhsh emerged into the light as from behind a curtain, and they found themselves in a peaceful place full of green, rolling hills and pleasant fields in which the young wheat was growing. The Sun was shining, and the air was very warm, and soon Rostam found that his clothing and helmet were soaked with sweat. Feeling the need for some rest, Rostam dismounted and took off Rakhsh's bridle so that he could graze. Then Rostam took off his helmet and his armor, which was made of a tiger's skin, and when his helmet and clothing had dried, he put the helmet and his armor back on and then lay down to sleep while Rakhsh nibbled on the shoots of fresh wheat.

Rostam had not been sleeping long when a man who had been set to guard the wheat saw Rakhsh wandering through the field and eating his fill. The man ran over to where Rostam lay and poked at his legs with a stick.

"You! Hey, you there! Wake up! Is that your horse? Why did you turn him loose there? Don't you know this is someone else's land? What makes you think it's all right to let your horse ruin a perfectly good crop? Get your horse and leave! You're not welcome here."

Rostam woke up, enraged at the man's words and at being unceremoniously poked with a stick. Rostam jumped up, grabbed hold of the man's ears, and then twisted them right off his head and threw them to the ground.

"You . . . you demon!" screamed the man. "You devil! You Ahriman in the flesh! How dare you! Wait until my master hears about this!"

Then the man picked up his ears and ran away.

Now, the servant who had been watching the wheat worked for a man name Olad. Olad was a fine young man of good family and had spent the day hunting with his friends. The servant ran up to Olad just as he was arriving home and inviting his friends inside for some wine. The servant showed his bloody ears to Olad and told him about the horrible man and monstrous horse ruining the wheat fields. Olad quickly remounted his horse, as did his friends, and they all rode off like the wind to see whom it was trampling Olad's crops.

When Rostam saw Olad and his friends riding toward him, he mounted Rakhsh and drew his glittering sword.

Olad reined in his steed before Rostam and said, "Tell me your name and who you serve. This is my land, and we don't let violent men do whatever they please here."

"My name is Rostam, and that name should freeze your blood. Surely, you've heard of me? You should know that no matter how many men you bring against me, you will never defeat me."

Then Rostam charged toward the group of young noblemen and began laying about him with his sword. Olad and his friends wheeled their horses around and fled, but not before several of the young men had been beheaded by Rostam.

Rostam gave chase on Rakhsh. As soon as he was within range, he took his lariat and lassoed Olad with it, pulling him off his horse. Rostam then jumped down and tied him up.

"Now, if you know what's good for you, you'll tell me what I want to know, and you'll tell me the truth. Tell me where I can find the White Demon and the demons Kulad Ghandi and Bid, and tell me where King Kavus and his army are being held prisoner. Do right by me, and I'll see that you're made king of Mazandaran when I'm done dealing with my enemies in that country."

Olad replied, "There's no need for violence. I'll tell you everything you want to know, and I'll tell you the truth. I'll show you where the White Demon is and how to get to where Kavus is. The demons dwell about one hundred parasangs from here. The place where Kavus resides is one hundred parasangs further on, and the entire two hundred parasangs is a journey full of peril. The whole place is crawling with demons led by Kulad Ghandi, with Bid and Sanjeh fighting at his side, and although you may think yourself quite fierce and warlike, you have nothing on the creatures that live in those places.

"Next, you'll have to pass through a land called Bargush, where all the people have dogs' heads, and if you thought Kulad Ghandi and his crew were bad, just wait until you see what awaits you on the other side of Bargush. There are six hundred thousand well-mounted soldiers there, all with the finest weapons and armor, and on top of that, there are twelve hundred war elephants. No one can survive running that gauntlet, not even the great Rostam."

When Rostam heard this, he laughed aloud. "That journey doesn't sound at all difficult. Anyway, when those demons see me coming, they'll all run away screaming, but it will be to no avail because I'll hunt down every last one of them and cleave them in two with my sword. And the ones I don't cleave, I'll crush with my mace. It's going to be a big job, so we'd better get started. Lead the way!"

The Sixth Trial: The Battle with Arzhang

Rostam and Olad rode onward all through the rest of the day and into the following night. When they arrived at the plain at the foot of Mount Aspruz, where the demons had defeated Kavus and his army, they could see the campfires of a great army in the distance ahead of them.

Suddenly, a great shouting and roaring went up into the night, and Rostam said to Olad, "What is this place? Who is making that terrible racket?"

"That is the camp of the demons who guard the border of Mazandaran. Kulad Ghandi is their leader, and the demons Arzhang and Bid are there too. The whole army has pledged their loyalty to the White Demon, and they're the ones making the noise," replied Olad.

"Right, we'll stop here for the night. This seems as safe a place as any. We'll get some sleep, but don't even think of running away if you value your life."

Rostam and Olad slept, and in the morning, Rostam tied Olad to a tree and took up his weapons. He mounted Rakhsh and set off toward Mazandaran, his helmet on his head and his tiger-skin armor on his body. On the way, he thought about how he might go about defeating his enemy and decided to look first for Arzhang and then see what he should do from there. When Rostam arrived at the edge of the demons' camp, he gave a great war cry. It was so loud that it echoed off all the mountains and split boulders in half.

Arzhang heard Rostam's cry and came rushing out of his tent to see who had made such a fearsome sound. Rostam saw Arzhang come out of his tent, so he urged Rakhsh into a gallop. Rostam roared into the demons' camp, and when he got close to Arzhang, he picked the demon up by the ears and ripped his head off with his bare hands. He then threw Arzhang's head to one side and his body to the other and drew his mace. The demons who had rushed to Arzhang's defense saw Rostam start to swing his mace and fled in terror. Rostam drew his sword and rode after them, laying about him first on one side and then on the other, until all the demons had either been slain or run into the mountains to hide.

The battle done, Rostam rode back to where he had made camp the night before and released Olad from the tree.

"Right, that's Arzhang and his crew dealt with. Now lead me to King Kavus," said Rostam.

Olad led Rostam to the city where the demons had housed the king and his army. As soon as they arrived on the outskirts, Rakhsh gave a great neigh that rang through the air.

Inside the city, Kavus said, "Did you hear that? That was Rakhsh neighing! Rostam is here, and soon we will be free!"

No sooner had Kavus said these words than Rostam rode up to him. The Persians all crowded around, cheering, and Kavus greeted Rostam with great joy.

"Oh, most welcome to you, Rostam! Never have you been so welcome to me. Come, tell us about your journey, and tell us how your father Zal is doing."

"My father is doing very well, O my king, except that he is greatly troubled by your plight and waits every day for word that you will be returning home. My journey has been long, but I have already killed Arzhang and many of his followers, and I hope to rid the earth of the rest of them before this is over," replied Rostam.

"I also await the day that I will return home, with much impatience, but that day will not come if you do not hurry and kill the White Demon as soon as you can. Once he hears of Arzhang's death, he will send swarms of his demon-soldiers out of the mountains, and there will be so many of them that even you, Rostam, will not be able to withstand them. To get to the White Demon's lair, you'll have to go into the mountains, which are all patrolled by demon soldiers. In the mountains, you'll find a great cavern that seems like nothing other than a black maw waiting to swallow you whole. That is where the White Demon lives. If you go into the cavern and kill him, the other demons will run away because they won't know what to do once they are leaderless.

"But listen, Rostam. We're more than just prisoners here—the demons have taken our eyesight. That's why they can put us in this city and not worry about guards. If you can, bring us back some of the White Demon's blood. Learned doctors have told us that this is the cure for our blindness if we use it as a balm on our eyes."

"I will leave right away, then. I'm going to track down this White Demon and destroy him, and hopefully, God will give me the strength I need. Otherwise, you'll have to languish here for who knows how long. But keep up your courage! I've never been defeated yet, and I'm sure that soon you'll be back home with your families."

The Seventh Trial: The Battle with the White Demon

Rostam readied himself for his battle with the White Demon and then rode toward the mountains with Olad as his guide. Soon enough, they could see the cavern Kavus had described and the many demon soldiers that stood between Rostam and the White Demon's lair.

Rostam said to Olad, "You have been faithful to your promise to tell me the truth. Now I ask you for the truth one more time. Tell me how I can get through those soldiers so that I can find the White Demon and kill him."

Olad replied, "You need to wait until noon when the Sun is highest and the day is warmest. The light and the heat make the demons go to sleep, and they'll be easy to conquer then. Be warned: A few of them are sorcerers, and they don't ever sleep at all. But if God is on your side, you should be able to defeat them easily."

Rostam took Olad's advice and waited until noon to ride to the White Demon's cave. When midday arrived, he tied Olad up with his lariat. Then he mounted Rakhsh, roared out his name so that all the mountains echoed with the sound, drew his sword, and rode forward to engage his foes. The demons never stood a chance, for Rostam rode through their ranks like a scythe through hay. He slashed off the heads of every single demon, and soon all of them lay dead.

Next, Rostam readied himself to enter the White Demon's cave. Never had Rostam seen a cave so dark and dank, and never had he faced such a fearsome enemy. He stood in front of the entrance to the cave for a moment, his heart racing with hope and fear. Then he stepped forward and peered into the shadows, trying to see his enemy. At first, he could see nothing but blackness, but after a time, a huge shape became visible within the darkness. Rostam continued staring at the shape, and soon he could make out a huge head of white hair atop a black body that was the size of a small mountain. Suddenly, the shape leaped at Rostam, and Rostam saw what it was: It was the White Demon, clad in armor like himself, ready and willing to do battle.

Rostam nearly quailed, for he had never seen any foe as large or strong or deadly. However, he summoned all his courage and slashed at the White Demon. His sword found its mark, lopping off one of the demon's legs at mid-thigh. This didn't stop the demon, though; wounded as he was, he propelled himself at Rostam, and soon the two of them were locked in close combat, rolling on the ground and punching and gouging at each other until the dust was so mixed with their blood that it turned into red mud. So strong and skilled was the demon that Rostam began to despair of his life.

But I can't stop now. Either I die here, or I kill this demon. Because if I run away, I have no hope of conquering Mazandaran. They'll all just laugh at me, he thought.

This thought gave Rostam new courage. He roared out his battle cry and threw the demon to the ground. Then, Rostam drew his dagger and slit the demon's throat, killing him. Rostam then cut the demon's heart and liver out of his body. When the whirl of combat was done, Rostam looked about him and saw, as if for the first time, how very large the White Demon was, and how very much blood he and his enemy had spilled.

Rostam rode back to the place where he had left Olad and released him from his bonds.

He handed the demon's liver to Olad, who said, "Never have I seen such a warrior as yourself. Even a lion would not have escaped from that combat alive. I now have hope that you will keep your word to me, and make me King of Mazandaran, for surely it would not be worthy of such a victor as yourself to go back on that promise."

Rostam replied, "I shall certainly keep my word to you and make you the king of this land. But before that can happen, we have many tasks to do and many battles to fight. There is the King of Mazandaran to deal with and hordes upon hordes of demons. But we will conquer, and then you will rule."

Rostam Returns to Kavus

Rostam and Olad rode back to the city where Kavus and his men were waiting.

Rostam went before the king and said, "O my king, hear now of my victory over the White Demon. I went into his cave and did dire battle with him, but in the end, I slit his throat and cut out his liver. What deed might I do next for your glorious majesty?"

"May you be forever and ever blessed, and may my kingdom never be without your aid and the might of your arm. And may your mother and father be forever blessed for giving my kingdom such a champion," replied Kavus.

Then, Rostam took some blood from the demon's liver and smeared it on Kavus's eyes, and the king's sight was restored. Rostam restored the sight of all of Kavus's soldiers, who then set up an ivory throne for their king.

Kavus sat upon the throne and held a council of war with Rostam and the army's generals, each one of them a mighty hero in his own right. When their plans were laid, the men held a great feast to celebrate their freedom and the defeat of the White Demon.

After a week of music, dancing, and wine, Kavus and his men put on their armor and took up their weapons. They went through the cities of Mazandaran as a raging fire goes through a field of dry grass.

Neither man nor woman nor child withstood the wrath of Kavus and his generals, but soon Kavus called a halt to the slaughter, saying, "We have meted out the punishment that this land deserves, so we will stop our pillaging for now. It is time to send a message to the King of Mazandaran, to give him a choice about whether he lives or dies, and about what befalls his country."

The First Letter to the King of Mazandaran

King Kavus summoned his scribe and told him to take down a letter on the finest white silk and perfume it with musk. This is what the letter said:

> *From Kavus, King of Persia, to the King of Mazandaran, greetings. We give thanks to God for having made the heavens and the earth and giving us the ability to choose between good and evil. If you follow the true faith and deal justly with your fellows, then everyone will call you blessed, but if you turn away from God and do evil, then evil surely shall befall you. Have you not seen what has befallen your soldiers? Have you not seen the fates of Arzhang, of Kulad Ghandi, of Bid, of the White Demon? You should know that the only way to save yourself is to give way to me and become one of my subjects because if you continue to resist, I shall have no choice but to loose the hero Rostam onto your kingdom, and there is no escape from the might of his arm. Bow to me, and pay Persia tribute, and you will live and continue to rule as King of Mazandaran. Defy me, and your fate will be the same as that of Arzhang, the White Demon, and every other demon that has been slain these past few days.*

When the letter was written and sealed, King Kavus gave it to one of his generals, a man named Farhad, who was known not only for his skill with a sword but also for his great probity.

"Take this letter to the King of Mazandaran, and we shall see whether he has any wisdom in that demonic head of his," said Kavus.

Farhad bowed to the king and then rode off to the land of the Gorgsaran, a place where the people's feet were made of leather, and the warriors fought with long, sharp daggers. This land was the place where the King of Mazandaran was residing at the time.

When the king heard that a messenger from Kavus was on his way there, the king sent three of his best warriors out to greet him.

"Go and meet this fellow, and mind you give him as much grief as you can. Provoke him into fighting with you. Do whatever it takes," said the king.

The warriors went to Farhad, looking as fierce and warlike as they possibly could. They tried harassing him with words, but Farhad remained cool and calm. When one of the warriors shook hands with Farhad, he squeezed so hard that many of Farhad's bones were broken, but Farhad made no sign that he felt any pain. The warriors gave up trying to provoke Farhad and brought him before their king.

"Welcome. I hope your ruler is doing well and that your journey was not too unpleasant," said the king.

"My king is well, thank you, and the journey was not arduous," said Farhad.

"Tell me your errand."

"I bring you a letter from King Kavus." Farhad handed the letter to the King of Mazandaran.

The king gave the letter to one of his scribes and said, "Read this aloud."

The scribe began to read, and when the king heard of the fates of Arzhang and the White Demon, his heart filled up with grief. When the king heard about the might of Rostam and his deeds, his grief mixed with rage. By the time the scribe finished reading, the king's eyes were filled with tears.

"Take silk and pen," the king said to the scribe, "and write down this reply to Kavus, the king of the Persians. 'To Kavus, King of Persia, from the King of Mazandaran, greetings. I have heard your letter and think you foolish to assume that your kingdom is more glorious than mine. I have an army of my own, and its might will overwhelm you. Every one of your warriors will be deprived of his head, and you will be utterly defeated.'"

When Farhad heard what the King of Mazandaran said, he did not wait to be given the letter. Instead, he mounted his horse and raced back to King Kavus.

Farhad told the king everything that had befallen him on his mission and related to him the reply that the king of Mazandaran intended to send. Rostam was there and heard everything Farhad said.

Rostam said to Kavus, "Send me to the king next. Write another letter, one that leaves no doubt about your warlike intent or the might of your army. I'll bring the letter and make some threats of my own."

Kavus agreed to this plan, saying, "Yes, let us do as you say. Even the King of Mazandaran will quail before you—neither man nor beast nor demon has yet been created who can withstand your strength and skill."

The Second Letter to the King of Mazandaran

When the scribe was ready with silk and ink, Kavus dictated this letter to the King of Mazandaran:

> *From Kavus, King of Persia, to the King of Mazandaran, greetings. I have read your letter and wonder how a man who should be wise stoops to saying such foolish things. Bow down to me as my subject. You have no other choice if you want to keep your life and your kingdom. Continue to defy me, and your kingdom will be mine anyway, and*

your rotting corpse will be left on the battlefield as food for the vultures.

The scribe wrote the letter, sealed it, and then gave it to Kavus. Kavus gave it to Rostam, who mounted Rakhsh and galloped away on his mission. The King of Mazandaran's guards saw Rostam approaching from afar.

One of them ran to tell the king the news. "O my king, another messenger from Kavus is on his way, but I've never seen his like. His shoulders are as broad as those of two men, and surely, he has the strength of a lion or maybe even an elephant. He has a fine lariat hanging from his saddle and a mace that even our mightiest warrior would struggle to lift. He is galloping here on a horse that is just as fearsome as he is."

The King of Mazandaran chose three of his best warriors and said, "Go out and greet this new messenger. You know what to do."

When Rostam saw the warriors coming to greet him, he dismounted Rakhsh near a large tree. Rostam pulled up the tree by its roots and waved it around as though it were a lance. Then Rostam threw the tree down and rode to meet the warriors, who had stopped in their tracks and gaped in astonishment at what Rostam was doing.

"Greetings! I come from King Kavus and have a message for the King of Mazandaran," said Rostam.

"Greetings to you. We have come to bring you to our ruler," said the chief warrior.

The warrior held out his hand for a handshake and attempted to crush Rostam's hand but found his own crushed instead by a smiling Rostam. So great was the pain that the warrior fainted and fell off his horse. The fall brought him back to consciousness, so he remounted and rode back with his companions to tell their king what had happened.

The king summoned a warrior named Kolahvar. Kolahvar was an expert horseman and the most skilled fighter in the whole kingdom. Everyone feared him because he was fierce as a leopard and liked nothing better than going to war and slaying his enemies.

The king said to Kolahvar, "Go out and meet this messenger. Show him what you're made of. Shame him so badly that he cries."

Kolahvar rode out to meet Rostam. He made himself look as fierce as possible and shouted many belligerent questions at the Persian hero. When Kolahvar finally decided to shake hands with Rostam, he squeezed so hard that Rostam's hand was badly bruised, but Rostam gave no sign that he felt any discomfort. In return, Rostam squeezed Kolahvar's hand so tightly that all his fingernails popped off. Kolahvar rode back to the king and showed him his useless hand.

"Look at what he did to me! If you have any wisdom at all, you'll give in and make yourself subject to the King of Persia. It's the best way to protect your people and yourself because there's no way we'll be able to stand against this warrior and Kavus's army," said Kolahvar.

Just as Kolahvar finished speaking, Rostam strode into the throne room and stood before the king.

The king asked him to be seated and then said, "So, you have come from Kavus? How is he faring? How fares his army?"

"Yes, my Lord. I am a messenger from King Kavus, who fares well, as does his army," replied Rostam.

"I heard about what you did to Kolahvarl. Surely you must be Rostam? No one else has that kind of strength."

"Oh, no, I'm not Rostam. I'm not even worthy of being his servant. He's much stronger and much more skilled than I am." Then Rostam gave Kavus's letter to the King of Mazandaran, saying, "Here is my ruler's reply to your foolish letter. You really should do the wise thing and capitulate. My sword rests uneasily in its sheath and longs to make its way through the necks of your warriors."

The King of Mazandaran was enraged by Kavus's letter and Rostam's bold words. "You go back to that so-called king of yours and tell him this: I will never bow to him as a subject, and I will pay him no tribute. Tell him that his overweening pride will be his downfall because he has goaded me beyond endurance. I will muster my army and attack him, and when I meet him face to face in battle, only one of us will be left standing, and that one will be me."

Rostam looked at the King of Mazandaran and his generals with disdain.

"Very well. You have sealed your doom," he said.

Then, he strode out of the hall and rode back to tell Kavus everything he had seen and heard.

"Don't worry about that fool and his army. They're no match for us. Let's get ready and make our battle plan. We have hordes of demons to destroy!" said Rostam.

The Battle Between the King of Mazandaran and the King of Persia

As soon as Rostam departed to return to Kavus, the King of Mazandaran began to muster his army and confer with his generals about their plan of attack. He had the royal pavilion packed to bring to the battlefield, and when his army was assembled and on the march, they put up so much dust as they went along that the mountains behind them were obscured, and the sky was darkened. That army was mighty and fearsome as besides warriors who went on foot and horseback, hundreds of war elephants were trained to fight just as fiercely as any human warrior.

A messenger told Kavus that the King of Mazandaran was approaching with his army, so Kavus summoned Rostam and his generals to make their plan of attack. When everyone agreed as to what was to be done, the army was assembled and the generals placed in command. They pitched their pavilions on the plain and arrayed their warriors according to their plan. Trumpeters blew their war fanfares, and the mountains rang with the sound. Kavus had such a large army that it seemed to be a forest of trees made of steel. King Kavus marched in the center of his army, while Rostam rode at the head.

When both armies had arrived at the plain, they halted, waiting for the battle to begin. But first, a great warrior from Mazandaran rode up to the Persian army. The warrior's name was Juyan, and he was the best fighter with a mace in his entire country.

Juyan rode back and forth in front of the Persians and shouted, "A challenge! Who will fight with me, champion to champion? Who will prove which is the mightier?"

The Persians heard Juyan's voice and saw how imposing he was, so none of them dared answer his challenge.

Kavus said, "Do you have blood in your veins or water? Are none of you true Persian men? Who will fight with this Juyan?"

When none of the Persian warriors replied, Rostam went to the king and said, "I'll fight him, your majesty. Let me do this deed."

Kavus replied, "The deed is yours. Go in victory."

Rostam took his lance and galloped onto the plain between the armies. He sent up a war cry that echoed off the mountains and made the whole battlefield shake.

Then, he called out to Juyan, "Who do you think you are, to challenge the army of the King of Persia? Go home, or else your mother will mourn you. Leave the service of the demon you call king—you are not worthy of the name of warrior otherwise."

Juyan said, "Bold words, but words don't frighten me. You should go home yourself. My dagger will turn your armor into shreds, and it is your mother who will be weeping."

When Rostam heard Juyan's words, he urged Rakhsh into a gallop. Rostam flung his lance as hard as he could at Juyan, and it hit him in the middle of his body. So hard did Rostam throw the lance that it went through Juyan's armor as though it were made of silk and was stuck there in the middle of his body, the head of the lance poking out through the warrior's back. Rostam rode up to Juyan and flung him to the ground, the lance still transfixing his body. The Mazandaran soldiers paled when they saw what Rostam did to Juyan.

The King of Mazandaran saw what was happening to his soldiers, so he shouted, "Men of Mazandaran! Have courage! We are the greater army, and our resolve is the strongest! Attack now! Victory to Mazandaran!"

War drums pounded and war trumpets blared on both sides as the armies advanced upon one another, and soon battle was joined. Swords flashed, steel clashed on steel, elephants brayed, and horses neighed as the two armies battered one another. Back and forth the battle went for a week, with neither army able to claim the victory.

When the eighth day dawned with no end to the war in sight, an exhausted Kavus took off his helmet and knelt on the battlefield.

"Lord God of the heavens, hear my prayer. If ever I have found favor in your eyes, grant me the victory over these demons," he said.

Then, Kavus put his helmet back on and mustered his army for yet another attack. Again and again, the Persians battered the Mazandaran forces. The Persian generals fought like lions, and Rostam seemed to be everywhere at once, demons falling at his feet like leaves from a tree in autumn.

Rostam and his companions fought their way toward the place where the King of Mazandaran was making his stand, but they could not break through the Mazandaran ranks. Rostam handed his lance to his squire and took up his mace instead. Wherever he struck with his mace, he dealt a death blow, whether to soldier or horse or elephant, and soon the ground around him was piled with corpses, and the Mazandaran army in rout—although the king and his companions still fought fiercely.

Rostam looked up and saw that he had a chance to kill the king. He took back his lance and hurled it with all his might. The lance went right through the king's armor and lodged itself in his spine, but instead of falling off his horse, dead, the king turned himself into a giant granite boulder, nearly as big as a small hill. Even Rostam was stopped in his tracks by this astonishing thing. Kavus saw Rostam standing there, agape, and rode up to him.

"Why are you standing there staring?" asked Kavus.

"I was in the midst of battle and working my way toward the King of Mazandaran. I laid about me with my mace and set the Mazandaran army into rout. Then, I took my lance and hurled it at the king. The lance transfixed his body, but instead of falling off his horse, he turned himself into this huge rock that you see before you."

Kavus ordered that the rock be taken back to the Persian camp. The strongest Persian men gathered around the rock and tried to pick it up, but they could not move it. Then, Rostam walked up to the rock, wrapped his arms around it, and with one great heave lifted it off the ground. He carried the rock back to the Persian camp while the Persian soldiers crowded around him, cheering. Rostam took the rock to the space in front of Kavus's pavilion and there set it down.

"Here is your enemy, O my king. What shall we do with him?" said Rostam.

Kavus stared at the great rock, still in awe at Rostam's feat. "I'm not sure what we can do. We don't have any demonic magic to turn him back into a man."

"Right, then I'll deal with him." Rostam turned to the rock. "Get rid of this silly disguise and face your fate like a man. If you don't, I'll get axes and crowbars and turn you into a big pile of pebbles."

The rock dissolved first into mist and then reformed itself as a trembling man clad in armor.

Rostam seized his arm and dragged him in front of Kavus, saying, "Look! Here is that boulder, that mighty crag, who quivers into mist when he hears about my ax!"

Kavus looked long at the King of Mazandaran and said, "I see nothing in you that would merit a kingdom. You are but a coward who played at being king." Then Kavus turned to his soldiers. "Take him away and execute him."

So, the King of Mazandaran was duly taken out of the camp and beheaded.

Kavus sent some of his soldiers over to the Mazandaran camp to see that any money, jewels, armor, or weapons were collected and piled into heaps. He then had all his soldiers come to him one by one to receive their payment, and to those who had suffered the most, he gave the most. Any demons who refused to acknowledge Kavus as king were taken away and executed. When all this work was done, Kavus went away from the camp and spent a week praying to God and thanking him for his victory. On the eighth day, he summoned anyone who might have need and gave generously to them out of his treasury.

Before returning home, Kavus declared a week of rejoicing.

"Let there be feasts and music and dancing, and let the wine flow freely! God has given us the victory, so let us celebrate!" he said.

Rostam went to the king during one of the feasts and said, "O my king, I wish to speak to you of Olad."

"Yes, tell me of him," said Kavus.

"I captured Olad and made him my guide. He was faithful and never led me wrong. We owe part of our victory to him. I promised him that he could be king of this land if we defeated Mazandaran, and I would like to keep my word to him."

"Yes, you certainly should keep your word. Bring Olad and the Mazandaran elders and chieftains before me tomorrow, and we shall give your friend his reward."

Thus, on the next day, the elders and chieftains of Mazandaran swore fealty to Olad, and Olad was crowned King of Mazandaran, subject to the King of Persia.

When all this was done, Kavus returned home to his kingdom.

Kavus's Homecoming and Rostam's Reward

Kavus's army marched home, triumphant to the sound of drums and trumpets. When the people saw that Kavus had returned, they streamed out of the city, cheering and singing his praises. The whole country gave itself up to rejoicing. Every place was full of the sound of music, and feast followed feast for an entire week.

The first thing Kavus did when he retook his throne was open the treasury and give sums of money to every household in his kingdom. For this purpose, he appointed special messengers and treasurers to ensure that everyone got their share. For Rostam, there were special gifts: A crown and throne of his very own, beautiful maidservants, fiery horses, rich clothing and jewelry, and sacks of gold and pearls. However, the greatest reward of all was the throne of Sistan.

Kavus crowned Rostam himself, saying, "Only a kingdom of your own is a fit reward since you restored to me my kingdom."

When all the festivities were over, Rostam returned to Sistan, where he ruled wisely and well.

Kavus, for his part, dispensed justice and mercy upon his people to the end of his days.

Part 2: Tales from the Caucasus

Captivating Myths and Legends from Circassia, Armenia, and Georgia

Introduction

The Caucasus Mountains straddle the isthmus between the Caspian Sea and the Black Sea. The region is at the crossroads of Europe, Central Asia, and the Middle East and is home to multiple cultures with rich histories and rich traditions. These cultures have produced unique myths and legends, which sometimes have taken on board elements from the traditions of the other nations, who, from time to time, have invaded and occupied this geographically strategic region. Although the Caucasus houses many distinct but related cultural groups, today, it is composed of the nations of Georgia, Azerbaijan, and Armenia, and its northernmost portion is part of the Russian Federation. Other Caucasian peoples include the Ossetians, Circassians, Abkhaz, and Chechens.

Various languages are spoken in this region that relate to three different language families. Georgian is a Kartvelian language spoken exclusively in the Caucasus; the Kartvelian languages are unrelated to any other language families. Azeri is a Turkic language spoken in Azerbaijan, while Armenian is an independent branch of the Indo-European language family that includes Slavic, Celtic, Indo-Iranian, and Romance languages.

The Caucasus region's mythology is a combination of native pagan traditions and influences from outside cultures, including ancient Greece and Persia. Christianity's and Islam's arrival also affected storytelling traditions, as did medieval knightly culture and medieval romance. ("Romance" in this sense refers to a lyric epic centered on the deeds of knights and romantic love.) Unfortunately, much Caucasian mythology and literature have been lost because of incursions by outside invaders: Russia engaged in a campaign of genocide in Circassia in the late nineteenth century, and Turkey did the same against the Armenians in the early twentieth. Once the region was absorbed into the Soviet Union, a considerable amount of native culture was purged as part of assimilation.

The oldest layer of myth from the Caucasus is comprised of the Nart sagas. Narts are a race of people around whom these myths are constructed and have many divine and semi-divine attributes. The Nart sagas tell the stories of the ancient Caucasian gods, and although the stories were altered in response to interactions with other cultures, you can still see the original traditions that inspired these myths. Nart sagas come from the northern part of the Caucasus but are not a unified corpus of myths. While the stories share a certain number of heroes, gods, and plots, each culture has its own names for the characters and versions of the tales, some of which are unique to a particular tradition.

The first part of this book contains myths and legends. Two of the stories in this volume are taken from the Circassian Nart corpus: "Sosruko's Sword" and "Tlepsh and Lady Tree." Sosruko is a Caucasian demigod and hero, known as Soslan in some other traditions; here, you have the story of some of Sosruko's childhood deeds. Tlepsh is an ancient Caucasian blacksmith deity associated with metal and metalworking, while Lady Tree would seem to be the embodiment of the world tree that holds all of creation together.

The influence of Persian mythology may be seen in the Armenian tale of Salman and Rostom. The hero Rostom would appear to be a version of the Persian Rostam, though this story is not connected to the Persian *Shahnameh* ("Tales of the Kings") in which the Rostam legends are contained. By contrast, the Armenian Rostom's cousin, Vyjhan, seems to be related to the character of Ohan in "David of Sassoun," the Armenian national epic. Like Ohan, Vyjhan is known for having a preternaturally loud voice.

"The Golden-Headed Fish" is one Armenian tale that has found audiences outside of the Caucasus. In the early twentieth century, folklorist Andrew Lang published a version of this tale in *Olive Fairy Book*.

The second part of this book presents versions of two national epics from the Caucasus. The first of these is a portion of the Armenian epic, "David of Sassoun." As with most hero tales, the protagonist has many superhuman qualities, but David also is very human; he makes mistakes and sometimes doesn't really understand how the world works, but he is committed to protecting the innocent from those who would harm them and is very concerned about establishing fairness, even if his idea of fairness goes against tradition. Full of the usual feats of strength, battles, magical armor, and magical creatures, "David of Sassoun" also revels in humor. We see this especially in David's relationship with his elderly neighbor, who provides him with tongue-lashings and vital information in equal portions, and in David's final battle with the evil Msrah Melik, who keeps asking for do-overs whenever his blows fail to kill David.

To end is an abridged version of the medieval Georgian national epic, "The Knight in the Panther's Skin." Written by poet Shota Rustaveli, "The Knight in the Panther's Skin" originally was a lyric epic in quatrains, participating in the medieval romance tradition. This tale was written after the advent of Christianity and Islam, and so is not part of the native mythological corpus as the tales about

Sosruko and Tlepsh. Nevertheless, it is a gripping story, a fairy tale on a grand scale, in which knights go on quests and pine for their lovers when they are parted, and in which a fair damsel is rescued from a tower. You also may see a faint hint of Persian influence in the person of the eponymous knight who, like Rostam, is clad in the skin of a great cat and carries a whip.

Each of these tales has its unique ethos and theme and contains an admixture of native Caucasian myth and connections to outside cultures and religions. They all show a different facet of Caucasian culture and beliefs about heroism, the pursuit of knowledge, loyalty, and love.

Section I: Myths and Folktales

Sosruko's Sword (*Circassia*)

The Nart Sosruko is among the most important heroes in Caucasian myth and legend. Like most heroes, he has an unusual birth. In some versions of the tale, he is born out of a rock (his name literally means "son of a stone") and then taken to the smithy of Tlepsh, the god of blacksmiths, to be finished. Sosruko has superhuman strength and preternatural growth; he is big enough to ride a horse by the time he is one year old.

When Sosruko was still a very young boy, he liked to visit Tlepsh at his forge, and Tlepsh was always happy to see him. One day, Sosruko went to Tlepsh's forge. Tlepsh was hard at work. "Greetings, Sosruko!" Tlepsh said. "My, how you've grown. You'll be almost as big as me soon, and I think you're old enough to help me at my work. Can you pump the bellows for me?"

Sosruko was proud that Tlepsh wanted his help. He went to the bellows and lifted the handle. When he pushed the handle down, the air came out in such a fierce stream that it blew away the fire, tools, and everything else that stood in its path. The only thing that did not move was the anvil because it was buried deep in the ground.

"That's enough of that, my lad. But I want to see how strong you really are. See if you can lift my anvil," Tlepsh said.

Sosruko tried, but he could barely budge the anvil.

"Ah, you still have some growing yet to do, I see. Never fear! You'll be strong enough one day," Tlepsh said.

Every day, Sosruko went to the forge and tried to lift the anvil whenever Tlepsh wasn't looking, and every day he was able to lift it a little bit further out of the ground. Finally, the day came when he was able to lift the anvil all the way up. He decided that he would surprise Tlepsh with this new feat of strength. He went to the forge very early in the morning, picked up the anvil, and put it in front of the forge door.

When Tlepsh arrived later to start his work, he said, "What is this here? Who moved my anvil? Who besides me is strong enough to do that?"

Tlepsh did not receive the answer to his question until the next day, when three young men, all of whom were Narts, came to the forge. One of the young men was carrying a scythe. Sosruko also was at the forge, watching Tlepsh at his work.

"Greetings," Tlepsh said to the visitors. "What brings you to my forge?"

"We want you to help settle an argument," the man carrying the scythe said. "This here is a magic scythe. It does all its work by itself. My brothers each say that the scythe should belong to them, but I say it should be mine. We don't want our quarrel to come to blows, so we hoped you could help us settle it."

"Yes, I will gladly help you. What do you want me to do?"

"Melt down the blade of the scythe and use the metal to turn it into a sword."

"Hm. I could do that, but I don't think your quarrel would end there. You'd just start fighting over the sword instead, and someone will get hurt."

"What other solution is there?" one of the brothers asked.

"How about this: I'll make you each a fine sword, and you give the scythe to me. I'll use the scythe to make a sword for Sosruko here."

"That's not what we want," the man holding the scythe said. "We want you to make a sword for us from this blade."

"I'll do it on one condition."

"Name it," the brothers said.

"I'll make the sword for whoever can lift my anvil and then put it back where it belongs. You can each have three tries."

Now, the young men were quite strong and very proud of it to boot.

Each of them thought, *Surely, I will be the one to lift the anvil and get that sword!*

The first brother laid hold of the anvil and pulled with all his might, but the anvil didn't move. He tried a second time, and a third, with no success.

The second brother took his turn and moved the anvil a little bit, but in his next two tries, he couldn't lift it any higher than the first time.

The third brother went to the anvil and gave a great heave. He was able to lift the anvil almost to his knees, but then he had to drop it. He tried a second and then a third time, but he could not lift the anvil the way Tlepsh told him he should, and now it lay on the floor, where the man had dropped it, out of its place.

"Well, I think that settles it," Tlepsh said. "The scythe is mine, and I'll make fine swords for each of you. Come back in three days. That's when your new swords will be ready."

"Yes, that is fair. We will come back then. Thank you for helping us," the brothers said.

Just then, Sosruko spoke up. "Tlepsh, can I try to lift your anvil?"

The three brothers looked at the young boy and all burst out laughing.

"You must be dreaming," the third brother said. "You're just a small child. How are you going to lift something that even grown men can barely get off the ground?"

"Yes. Why don't you go back home to your mama? Come back when you're a man," the second brother said.

"Don't even try it. You'll surely hurt yourself," the first brother said.

Sosruko listened to the men's laughter and the rude things they said to him. It made him very angry. He stomped over to the anvil and put his arms around it. He picked it up, set it back in the hole where it belonged, and then pushed until the anvil was all the way into the earth and the top of it was level with the forge floor.

Tlepsh, at first, was astonished but then laughed. "Well done, young Sosruko! Now I think I know who moved my anvil yesterday morning!"

The three brothers also wondered at Sosruko's feat. "Well done indeed, little lad! You have well earned a magic sword, and when you grow up, you can be a champion for the Narts!"

Tlepsh and Lady Tree (*Circassia*)

In this story, the smith god Tlepsh goes on a journey, looking for knowledge. He doesn't find what he seeks but learns some other important lessons instead.

In his collection of Nart sagas, translator John Colarosso notes the cosmic import of both Lady Tree and the child she bears to Tlepsh. The child himself is the Milky Way, which is high in the sky only at certain times of the year, while Lady Tree herself is a world tree, a mythical concept shared with cultures such as the ancient Norse and the ancient Maya. Colarosso further observes that the ancient people who made the myth about Tlepsh and Lady Tree might have thought of the Milky Way as a kind of baby sun and that the seven women tasked with looking after Tlepsh's child might represent the Pleiades.

One day, Tlepsh sat moping in his forge. He was trying to think of something new he could make, but he had no ideas.

"I know how to make sickles and scythes, swords and knives, but what else is there? I'm tired of making those things, but I don't know what else there is to make," Tlepsh said.

Just then, Lady Satanaya came walking past the forge.

That's it! I'll ask the Lady. She is very wise. Tlepsh thought.

Tlepsh called out to Lady Satanaya and invited her into the forge. "My Lady, I have a problem, and since you are so very wise, maybe you can help me solve it."

"Maybe," the Lady said, who didn't really want to be there; she was on an errand and in a hurry. "Tell me what you need."

"I want to make something new in my forge, but I have no ideas. Can you think of some things I might make?"

"I'm not sure why you think I can help you. I think you already make plenty of things. Sickles and scythes and swords and knives are very useful, you know."

"Yes, I know that, but I'm bored with making those. What should I do?"

"Well, maybe you should go on a journey. Go to new lands and meet new people. Maybe if you see what they do in other countries, you'll get some ideas."

"Oh, that's a grand plan, thank you! But I've never traveled before. I don't know what I should take with me."

"I don't think you need to worry about food. Everyone knows you and will be glad to share what they have. Wear a good suit of clothes that won't tear or go threadbare easily and a pair of stout shoes. That's really all you need."

"Thank you, my Lady. I'll start right away!"

Tlepsh then made himself a good pair of boots from the finest steel. He slipped them on and started his journey.

Tlepsh was very fast. He could go as far in one day as a normal man could go in a month, and he could go as far in one month as a normal man could go in a year. Tlepsh went on and on, over mountains and across rivers, until he finally came to the sea. He hadn't found what he was looking for yet, so he decided to see whether the people on the other side of the water might help him. He went into the nearby forest and uprooted some trees with his bare hands. He tied them together to make a raft and then pushed the raft into the surf.

After a time, he came to a new land he had never seen before. He beached the raft and went ashore. On the grass just above the beach, a group of beautiful maidens was playing a game. Tlepsh had never seen such beautiful young women. Each of them was perfectly formed, with lovely flowing hair and beautiful voices like musical bells. Tlepsh decided that he must have one of those women for himself, so he ran across the beach and tried to catch one of the girls, but she slipped out of his grasp, laughing. Tlepsh tried to catch one girl after another, but no matter how quickly he moved, they always seemed to be able to get away from him.

Finally, Tlepsh stopped chasing the maidens. "Please, have pity on me and tell me who you are."

"We are the maidens who serve Lady Tree. You have to ask the Lady's permission before you can have one of us. We'll take you to see her now," the girls said.

The maidens led the way, and Tlepsh followed them. Soon they came to a strange being.

"This is Lady Tree. You may speak to her," the maidens said.

Tlepsh looked at Lady Tree. He had never seen anyone like her before. She looked something like a tree and something like a woman, and a very beautiful woman at that. Her roots went deep, deep, deep into the earth, and her hair reached up into the heavens. She had two lovely, maidenly arms and a delightful face.

When Lady Tree beheld Tlepsh, she immediately fell in love with him. She invited him into her house and fed him a good meal. Then, she showed him a place with a soft bed. Tlepsh was very tired from his long journey, so he fell asleep almost at once.

In the small hours of the night, Tlepsh started awake to find Lady Tree standing next to his bed, gazing at him. Tlepsh found her very beautiful, and he desired her. He stood up and tried to put his arms around her, but Lady Tree stepped back.

"Stop! You must not touch me. I am not for a mortal man," Lady Tree said.

"But I am not a mortal man. I am a god."

Then Lady Tree and Tlepsh made love and were very happy.

In the morning, Tlepsh made to leave.

"Don't go! Please stay with me. I love you!" Lady Tree said.

"I must go. I am journeying to find knowledge to bring back to the Narts. I'm going to journey to the end of the earth because that is where the knowledge might be found."

"You don't need to go anywhere to get that knowledge. I have all the knowledge you could ever want right here. My roots go down, down, down to the very center of the earth and always bring secrets back to me. My hair goes up, up, up to the very highest heaven, and I can teach you anything you might want to know about what there is in the skies."

"Maybe, but what I need is the knowledge from the end of the earth."

"This is where you are wrong. The earth has no end. No matter how far you travel, you will never find it. Stay here with me, and gain the knowledge that you seek!"

The Lady pleaded and pleaded with Tlepsh, but he would not listen. He put on his steel shoes and set out on his journey, leaving Lady Tree weeping behind him.

Tlepsh journeyed on and on and on until the soles of his shoes were nearly worn through, but still, he did not come to the end of the earth. He was wearied from his travels and so turned his path back to the home of Lady Tree.

When he arrived, she was there to greet him.

"So, did you find the end of the earth?" the Lady asked.

"No," Tlepsh replied.

"Did you learn anything in your travels?"

"Yes, that the earth has no end."

"Did you learn anything else?"

"Yes, that a man's body can be hard as steel."

"What else did you learn?"

"That the longest, hardest road is the one you have to travel all by yourself."

"Those are good things to have learned, but what of the knowledge you wanted to bring back to the Narts? Did you find that?"

Tlepsh sighed. "No, I didn't find that anywhere. I looked and looked, but it was nowhere to be found."

"That is unfortunate, and it is unfortunate that you did not stay when I asked you to. If you had stayed, I could have taught you everything you wanted to know, everything that you were seeking on your journey. I even could have taught you how to live forever. But now it is too late, and someday you will die. Even so, I have a gift for you." Lady Tree put a tiny infant sun into Tlepsh's arms. "This is the child you gave me before you left. Guard it well and watch it grow. When it is fully grown, it will teach you all the things you want to know."

Tlepsh returned home with his infant son. He showed the child to the Narts.

"Look up into the night sky. Do you see the Milky Way there?" Tlepsh said.

"Yes, we see it," the Narts replied.

"Whenever you go out on a raid, keep it in sight. Then you'll never get lost."

The Narts promised to heed Tlepsh's words. They found seven women to look after the child.

One day, the child went out to play and disappeared. The women noticed he was missing. They searched everywhere but could not find him.

"The child is missing! You must find him!" they told the Narts.

The Narts saddled their horses and went looking for the child, but they had no luck.

"Maybe the child went back to his mother's house. You're the only one who knows the way. Go and look for the child there," they told Tlepsh.

Tlepsh went to the home of Lady Tree, but his child was not there.

"What do we do now?" Tlepsh asked.

"There is nothing you can do. You will just have to wait until he comes back of his own accord. And when he comes back, you will find yourself fortunate. But if he stays away forever, that will be the end of you," Lady Tree replied.

Tlepsh returned home, mourning the loss of his child.

Salman and Rostom *(Armenia)*

This story of a single combat between two fearsome warriors reflects historical ties between Armenia and Persia and functions as a just-so story about the origins of earthquakes and thunder. The hero of this tale, Rostom, clearly is the Persian hero of the same name (Persian Rostam*), and Rostom's father, Chal, clearly is the Persian Zal. The story retold below is unconnected to the Rostam cycle in Ferdowsi's* Shahnameh*; here, Rostom has been co-opted as an Armenian fairytale hero.*

A long time ago, a giant named Salman was the terror of all the lands around. He forced all the people to pay him tribute. If a town or city could not or would not pay the tribute, Salman would go there and kill all the people, destroy their homes and barns, and lay waste their fields.

The only person who dared to refuse to pay Salman was a nobleman named Chal. Chal was very big and strong, but he looked small compared to his son, Rostom. Rostom was a giant of a man and so strong that he could pull whole trees up by their roots. There was only one horse in the whole world who could carry Rostom. This horse was a magical steed who had white hooves.

One day, Chal decided that he would go and see what Salman had been up to. He mounted his horse and set off to look for Salman. Chal journeyed here and there, but he didn't find Salman until, one day, he saw a huge man mounted on a huge horse coming his way up the road. The man had an enormous spear and looked very fierce indeed. Now, Chal had never seen Salman before, so he did not know that this was the person he had been seeking. Nevertheless, Chal was never one to turn down an opportunity to fight, so he set his spear in rest and charged at the huge man. The giant spurred his horse toward Chal, but instead of engaging his spear, he rode right past as though Chal wasn't even there.

Chal was furious. He had never been so insulted. He turned his horse around and threw his spear with all his might at the giant. The spear whizzed past the giant's head, at which the giant turned around, galloped toward Chal, and plucked Chal out of his saddle as though he were a rag doll. Then the giant bound Chal to the belly of his horse and rode for home.

The giant lived in a huge tent that was pitched near a river. He brought Chal inside the tent and nailed his ear to the tent pole. Then Salman went to his bed, laid down, and went to sleep.

Chal was nearly blind with rage.

"He didn't even have the courtesy to tell me who he is," he muttered to himself.

Salman didn't sleep long. When he woke, he said to Chal, "Tell me who you are."

"I am someone from Chal's country," Chal said, thinking it wise not to reveal his true name.

"Oh, that's good." Salman released Chal from the tent pole. "That means you can go to Chal and tell him to send his son Rostom to fight me. I've heard stories about Rostom, and I want to see which of us is stronger. Tell Chal and Rostom that it is Salman who asks this."

Chal went home. He cast himself down in a chair and sighed.

Rostom noticed his father seemed downcast. "What is wrong, father? What happened on your journey?"

"Well, I found Salman all right. The brigand captured me and nailed my ear to the pole of his tent. He told me that he wants to fight you to see who is stronger. He doesn't know I'm your father. I gave him a false name."

"If Salman wants a fight, then he'll have one. He shall pay for the insult he did to you."

Rostom made ready for his journey. He invited his cousin, Vyjhan, to come along. When it was time to leave, Rostom bade farewell to his horse.

Rostom said to Chal, "If I am in any danger, my horse will know and will stamp his hooves. When he does that, tie all my weapons to his saddle and let him come to me."

Rostom and Vyjhan disguised themselves as wandering monks and set off on their journey. Now, just as Rostom was both huge and strong, Vyjhan also was very large, but his strength was in his voice, not his arms. If Vyjhan cried out, people could hear him on the other side of the country, even if mountains stood in the way.

Vyjhan and Rostom traveled all through that day, and when the sun began to set, they made camp near a small town. In the middle of the night, Vyjhan was awakened by the noise of people lamenting. He went into the village and there saw all the people crying and tearing their clothes.

Vyjhan went up to one of the villagers and asked, "What has happened? Has someone died? Has some disaster overtaken you?"

"The disaster hasn't happened yet, but it will soon. We owe tribute to the giant Salman. We haven't paid it for seven years, but just now he told us we have to have the whole amount ready by morning or he'll kill us all and destroy our village!" the villager replied.

The people worked very hard, and by daybreak, the tribute was ready. Vyjhan saw them arguing over who should be the one to give Salman the tribute. No one wanted to do it because Salman took both the tribute and the person giving it, and the person was never seen again.

"Why don't you let me give the tribute? I'm not afraid," Vyjhan said.

Soon enough, Salman came to the village. He collected all the tribute and scooped up Vyjhan along with it. He took Vyjhan to his tent and nailed his ear to the tent pole.

Vyjhan called out, "Rostom! Help! Salman has captured me!"

Vyjhan's loud cry woke Rostom from sleep. Rostom ran to the village and asked what happened.

"Salman took your friend to his tent by the river. Don't bother to go after him. There's no way Salman can be defeated. Mourn your friend and go home," the villagers said.

No sooner had the villagers told Rostom their tale than Rostom's faithful horse galloped to his side. The horse was saddled, and all of Rostom's weapons and armor were there. Rostom put on his armor, mounted his horse, and galloped to the river.

When he arrived at Salman's tent, he shouted, "Salman! Come out and face me! It is I, Rostom. Let us see who is stronger!"

Salman came out of the tent armed and ready for battle. The two giants fought with spears until nothing was left of the shafts but splinters. Then they drew their swords and fought until their shields were cut to ribbons and their swords were shattered. When all their weapons were broken, they grappled and wrestled this way and that, but neither one could get the upper hand.

Salman and Rostom are still wrestling today. When one of them throws the other, it makes the ground shake, and Vyjhan's booming call can still be heard from time to time throughout the world.

The Golden-Headed Fish (*Armenia*)

This Armenian folktale does not deal with ancient gods or heroes but is closer to a fairy tale, following the adventures of a disgraced prince accompanied by a magical being. This story's function is entertainment, but it also has a strong moral core on the virtues of mercy, loyalty, and repayment of debt.

There once was a king who found his eyesight failing. All of the most learned doctors from all corners of the kingdom were summoned to treat the king, but none could find a cure. Word came to the king that one doctor in a far country was even more learned than all of those in the whole kingdom put together.

"Go and fetch this doctor. Bring him here straight away. He is my last hope," the king said.

The messengers found the doctor and brought him back to the king's court.

The doctor examined the king and said, "There is a cure for your malady. It requires the blood of the golden-headed fish. If I smear some of that on your eyes, you will see again. I will stay here for one hundred days. If by the end of that time you have not found the fish, I must go back to my home."

Now, the king only had one child, a son, who loved his father dearly. The prince had been at his father's bedside when the doctor told the king what the cure could be. The prince begged for the opportunity to go fishing, for he wanted to be the one to restore his father's sight if he could. The king gave permission, and soon the prince and his companions had put to sea.

Day after day, they cast their nets, and day after day, they failed to catch the fish. Ninety days came and went, and then ninety-eight, and on the ninety-ninth day, they fished and fished until the sun was nearly setting, and still no golden-headed fish. The prince and his companions were downcast.

One of the companions said, "I think this task is impossible. Maybe that doctor was telling a story to make fools of us and his majesty the king. We should go home before it gets dark."

"Maybe you're right, but I'll not turn for home until we've cast our nets one last time. Maybe we'll be lucky," the prince said.

And so, the prince and his companions cast their nets and hauled them back in again, and what should they find among the catch but a golden-headed fish! The men placed the fish inside a barrel full of water and put the barrel in the prince's cabin. Then they sailed for home, singing all the way.

While they were sailing home, the prince went to look at the marvelous fish. He gasped with astonishment when the fish put its head above the water and began to speak.

"I know you are a prince. I am a prince too. Please throw me back into the sea. You will have a great reward if you save my life," the fish said.

The prince wavered, but the fish pleaded in such piteous tones and gazed at him with such piteous eyes that the prince took the fish out of the barrel and tossed it back into the sea.

The prince's friends saw what he had done and cried out, "What are you doing? We fished for ninety-nine days to catch that fish! What is your royal father going to say?"

But the prince would only answer, "I have my reasons," and said no more.

When the prince and his companions arrived back at the palace, the companions told the king what the prince had done.

"How dare you! How dare you take from me the one chance I had for a cure. Tomorrow I will hang you as a criminal! You are no son of mine!" the king shouted.

The queen heard what the king said, so she quickly spirited the prince away and put clothes on him that made him look like a commoner. She gave him a purse full of gold and jewels and sent him to the harbor to find passage on whichever ship was sailing farthest away. With many tears, mother and son bid farewell to one another, and soon the prince was at sea again, thinking that, this time, he would never return.

The prince disembarked on the distant island the ship brought him to. He found a pleasant cottage to live in and soon desired a servant to wait upon him. He sent out word that he was looking for such a servant, and the next day, there was a line of men outside his door hoping to get the position. The prince interviewed one after the other, and at the end of the interview, he asked them what wages they desired. Everyone answered with a sum of money that they said must be paid at the end of every month. Although the prince thought that any one of the men would do as a servant, he also had the nagging feeling that he hadn't found the right man yet, so he continued interviewing one man after another.

At the end of a very long day, there was finally only one candidate left.

The prince spoke with him about his qualifications, and as he had done so many times before, he said, "What do you expect for wages?"

"I don't need to be paid, sir, at least not yet. Let me serve you for a time, and if you think me worth paying, you can reward me then," the man replied.

The prince was intrigued by this and told the man that he was hired.

The two lived together peaceably for a time, but then one day, terror came to their little island. A dragon took up residence not far away, and it had begun raiding cattle pens and sheepfolds.

"What shall we do? Once the dragon eats all our sheep and cattle, it will eat our children, and then it will surely eat us!" the people lamented.

The king of the island sent some soldiers on an expedition to kill the dragon. When none of them came back, he sent another group of soldiers, and then another, and then another, but none of them came back alive. In despair, the king proclaimed that anyone who killed the dragon would get half his kingdom and the hand of his daughter in marriage.

The servant heard the proclamation. Without saying anything to the prince, he went to the palace and asked for an audience with the king.

"My master can kill that dragon. Will you keep your word and reward him as you said?" the servant said.

"I most certainly will. That dragon has already eaten half my army. Anyone who can kill that beast deserves that kind of reward," the king replied.

That night, the servant slipped quietly out of the house and went to the place where the dragon lived. When it came slithering out of its den, the servant killed it and then cut off its ears. He took the ears home with him and woke the prince.

"Take these to the king. Tell him you killed the dragon. He'll give you half his kingdom and his daughter in marriage," the servant said.

"But I didn't kill the dragon. You did. The reward should be yours," the prince said.

"Never mind that. Just do as I say, and everything will go well for you."

The prince did as his servant suggested. He brought the ears to the king, who immediately gave him half his kingdom and his daughter in marriage.

The prince and his wife soon had a fine son, and when the old king passed away, the prince was made ruler over the whole island.

One day, the servant went to the prince and said, "Sir, we should make another journey. Abdicate your throne in favor of your son. Make your wife regent. She is wise and will rule well. Then we sail for the Kingdom of the West. More good fortune awaits you there."

The prince did as his servant said, reluctantly saying farewell to his wife and child.

The two men set sail, and after a few days at sea, they arrived at the Kingdom of the West.

"Go to the palace and ask the king for his daughter's hand in marriage. She is the most beautiful woman in the world and will make you a fine wife," the servant told the prince.

The prince duly went to the palace and asked for an audience with the king.

When the king heard that the prince wanted to wed his daughter, he said, "You seem like a fine young man, and I'm sure you'd make a good husband for my daughter. But you should know that I have already tried ninety-nine times to wed my daughter, and every time, the poor young man dies on the wedding night. You can marry her as well if you like, but don't say I didn't warn you."

At first, the prince balked at marrying the king's daughter, but the servant reassured him.

"Never fear. It will all go well in the end. I'll see to that," he said.

The next day, the prince and princess were wed in a sumptuous ceremony. When the wedding feast was done, the young couple retired to their chamber. The prince was horrified to see that a coffin and a shroud had already been prepared and were waiting at the foot of the bed.

"What is this for?" the prince asked his bride.

"I'm sure my father told you the story. Some time ago, they decided to keep one of those in my chamber to save the trouble of making one on the morning after my weddings. I know it's strange, but you did know the danger when you agreed to marry me," the princess replied.

The young people went to bed and soon were asleep.

Now, during the wedding banquet, the servant had excused himself, saying that he wanted to be sure everything was ready in the bridal chamber, but what he really wanted to do was find a place to hide. He armed himself with a pair of tongs and a sharp dagger and then secreted himself into a wardrobe and waited until the prince and his bride were asleep. The servant eased the wardrobe door open and crept to the edge of the bed. The princess opened her mouth in her sleep, and what should come slithering out but a long, black viper! The servant grabbed the viper with the tongs and sliced off its head. He took the weapons and the serpent's body and buried them in the castle gardens.

In the morning, some men came into the bedchamber. The king had sent them to deal with the prince's dead body, but when they entered the room, they found that the prince was quite alive, sitting in bed and chatting with his wife over a breakfast prepared by the prince's servant. The king was overjoyed to see that the groom had lived out his wedding night.

"This marriage surely will be blessed. My daughter finally has a husband who can love her for all her days," he said.

The prince and his bride lived happily in the palace for a time, but soon the old king died. Since the king had no male heir, the prince took his throne. He ruled the kingdom well for some years until, one day, a messenger came to his court.

"I have been sent by your royal mother. Your father is dead. You've inherited his kingdom. Please come home at once," the messenger said.

The prince found a regent to rule in his stead and then took ship with his wife.

On the way, they stopped at the island to fetch the prince's first wife and his son. Then they sailed for his father's kingdom. They were welcomed with great rejoicing, and soon the prince and his family had made their home in the palace. Thus, the prince became lord not only over his father's kingdom but also of the island and the Kingdom of the West.

One day, the servant came to the prince and said, "Sir, you have two beautiful wives, a goodly kingdom, and vast treasure. My time with you is done. I must return to my home."

The prince was saddened to hear this. "Can't I persuade you to stay? You have advised me and served me well, and I am very grateful."

"No. I really must go."

"Very well, but take any amount of my treasure with you. All I have is yours, for I would have none of it at all if it weren't for you. You saved my life."

"I require no treasure, for I was only repaying my debt to you. You see, I am the golden-headed fish."

Section II: National Epics

David of Sassoun (*Armenia*)

"David of Sassoun" is the Armenian national epic. It covers the history of four generations of the same family, starting with the twin brothers Sanasar and Baghdasar, who are miraculously conceived when their mother drinks water from a magic spring. Like many heroes conceived by magic or miracle, Sanasar and Baghdasar are larger than life, have superhuman strength, and own a supernatural and immortal horse named Kourkig Jelaly ("Majestic Horse"). Many of the brothers' qualities are passed down from generation to generation, including to their grandson David, the eponymous hero of the epic. The story is set in Sassoun, which today is the district of Sason in the Batman Province of Southeastern Turkey—although historically, this area was Armenian territory, and according to the epic, was founded by Sanasar and Baghdasar themselves.

One focus of this story is the conflict between the Christian Armenians and their Muslim occupiers, reflecting historical truth. In the seventh century, Armenia was a province of the Umayyad Caliphate, and in the eleventh century, Armenia was invaded by the Muslim Seljuk Turks. The epic itself opens on a scene of conflict between Armenians and invading Muslims, in which the king of Armenia is forced to give his daughter, Dzovinar, to the Muslim

Caliph as part of a peace treaty. When Dzovinar conceives Sanasar and Baghasar, the Caliph is furious and plots to kill Dzovinar and her children. The boys evade execution and eventually rescue their mother from the Caliph's clutches, and so begins the tale of their dynasty.

We also see how Persian culture intermingled with Armenia in the characters of the devs, evil demon-like beings who steal some of David's cattle. Devs originally were creatures from Persian mythology but were eventually adopted into the mythologies of surrounding nations, including Armenia.

Because the entire epic is too long for this present volume, only a brief part is included here, and it has been rendered in prose rather than in its original poetic form. We join the story after the death of Sanasar's son, Medz ("Lion") Mher. Mher's wife then dies of grief, leaving their young son, David, an orphan. The crosscurrents between Armenians and their Muslim occupiers continue in this part of the epic, with the conflict between David and the Arab Msrah Melik, whose name means "king of Msr." Most translators render Msr as "Egypt," but in his translation of the epic, Artin Shalian says that "Msr" actually refers to a place in ancient Assyria.

David the Herdsman

When David was but a lad, he got into trouble so often that the townspeople begged his uncle Ohan to give him some occupation.

Ohan went to the boy and said, "Dear David, how would you like to herd the people's sheep and goats?"

"Yes, I think I'd like that. How do I do it?" David replied.

"You take the animals up to the pasture in the morning and drive them back home in the evening."

"Very well, but I'll need new shoes."

Ohan went to the blacksmith and had him make a pair of steel boots and an iron crook for him to use in herding the sheep. David was very pleased with his boots and crook and couldn't wait for morning to come so that he could start his work.

Finally, the new day dawned. David went to all his neighbors and offered to take their flocks out to pasture. The people all agreed, and soon David was in charge of a great flock of sheep and goats. He herded them up into the hills so that they could graze. When it came time to take the animals back home, he noticed that they were scattered about the hills.

What shall I do? I have to bring them all back, David thought.

David immediately went to work rounding up all the sheep and the goats, but in his enthusiasm, he also rounded up martens and ermines, pheasants and rabbits, and even a few foxes and placed them among the animals belonging to his neighbors. When the people of Sassoun saw David returning not only with goats and sheep but a great number of wild animals, they became afraid and hid in their homes.

"What have you done?" Ohan asked when he saw the motley herd David was driving through the town.

"I gathered up all the beasts and am bringing them home. I even found a few more to add to the flock," David replied.

"Yes, but only some of those are sheep and goats. The rest are wild animals."

Then Ohan had to show David how to tell the sheep and goats from the other creatures, and when the people stopped being afraid, they took the martens and ermines and foxes and used their skins to make fine furs for the winter, and they ate the pheasants and rabbits for their dinners.

The next day, the people went to Ohan and said, "Your nephew didn't exactly cause a disaster yesterday, but we don't want him herding our flocks anymore. Give him something else to do."

Ohan said to his nephew, "The people don't want you herding their sheep and goats anymore. How about you take the cattle up to the pasture instead?"

"Yes, I'll do that, Uncle, but I need a new pair of shoes. I already wore out the ones you gave me the other day," David replied.

So, Ohan had the blacksmith make David another pair of steel boots, and in the morning, David collected the cattle and brought them up to the pasture. This time, though, his uncle made sure to tell him only to bring back the animals he was taking up in the morning and to take nothing that looked different from the animals in his herd. David soon learned to herd the cattle well, and they prospered under his care. David also made friends with other herdsmen, and they watched their animals together.

One day, David and his friends were taking the cattle out to pasture as usual when David saw many people going toward the church.

"Where are they going?" David asked.

"It's a holy day today. They're going to church, and then afterward, they will eat and celebrate," one of the herdsmen replied.

Another herdsman said, "I wish I could eat and celebrate, too. That stew they make for the festival, it's so good!"

"If you watch my cattle, I'll go and get some stew for all of us," David said.

The herdsmen agreed, and so David set off for the church.

At the church, David found the women preparing several cauldrons of delicious-smelling stew.

"Greetings. May I have some stew to take back to my friends? We are herding everyone's cattle, and so can't come to the celebration," David said.

"No, you certainly may not have any stew," one of the women replied.

"But my friends and I are hungry, and I see here that you have plenty."

"Even so, you may not have any."

"We'll see about that."

David took his oaken staff and thrust it through the rings of one of the cauldrons. Then he picked up the cauldron, using the staff for a handle. He grabbed a few loaves of bread from a nearby table and started walking back to where his friends were waiting.

"Now, wait just one minute! Come back with our stew!" one of the women cried.

Just then, the priest came out of the church. He saw David walking off, carrying the enormous cauldron full of stew with only one hand.

"Hush, Mother. Don't you see that he's one of those men from Sassoun? That he's Medz Mher's son? Don't make him angry, or he'll come back and kill us all. We still have plenty for everyone else. Let it be," the priest said.

David strode back to the pasture, where he found his friends standing uneasily in a group.

David put down the cauldron and said, "Hey, boys, come and eat! Doesn't this smell good? I brought us some bread, too." When the other men didn't move or say anything, David added, "What's gotten into you? I went all the way to the church to get this, and now you won't eat it?"

"It's not that, David. It's that while you were gone, forty terrible devs came and drove off our cattle," one of the herdsmen said.

"Did they, now? Well, I'll not tend to forty devs on an empty stomach. Come on, let's eat, and then I'll go get our cattle back."

After David and the herdsmen had eaten their fill, David said, "Tell me which way the devs went."

The herdsmen showed him, and so David followed the tracks of the cattle up into the mountains. The tracks went into a cave from which smoke was issuing. David peered inside the cave, and there were the forty terrible devs. The devs had already slaughtered the cattle, skinned them, and put the meat on to boil in a huge cauldron. When he saw this, David was enraged. He roared a roar so loud that all the devs were quaking.

"That was Medz Mher's son for sure. Quick, go and pacify him before he kills us all," the chief of the devs said.

The devs went to speak with David, but he beheaded them with his staff one by one until none were left alive. Then David went into the cave, where he found the kettle full of meat, a pile of hides, and a great mountain of treasure. There was also a great stallion tied to a ring in one wall. David dumped the meat out of the kettle and filled it with treasure. Then he picked up the hides and the kettle full of treasure and went back to the village, where he distributed the wealth and arranged for the cattle owners to give the hides to those who needed them most. The kettle he gave to the women at the church, in exchange for the one he had taken earlier.

David went home to fetch his uncle and tell him about the treasure.

"Bring some asses to carry the loot. Even I can't carry all that by myself," David said.

David and his uncle went up to the cave. When the uncle saw the devs' headless bodies, he went nearly as white as snow and started to run away.

"Why are you running? They're dead. They won't harm anyone anymore," David said.

The two men went into the cave.

When Ohan saw the treasure and the horse, he said, "Oh! This is Medz Mher's treasure and his horse! The devs have been stealing this since he died."

"I'll give you all the treasure if you give me the horse. And I warn you to do as I ask, or I will have to hurt you," David said.

"The treasure and the horse all belong to you. I don't want any of it."

"I have no use for the treasure. Bring it home and give it to everyone in the town. I only want the horse."

And so, Sassoun became very wealthy, and all the people were happy.

David Rebuilds His Father's Monastery

One day, not long after he defeated the devs, David bought a hunting falcon and then rode his horse out to see whether his falcon might catch any birds for him. David was intent on his hunt, so he didn't pay attention to where he was riding. He ended up in a millet field, and his horse's hooves churned all the furrows to mud and crushed the young shoots of millet.

The old woman who owned the field came hobbling out of her house and shouted at David. "You there! What do you think you're doing, trampling my fine millet? If you want to hunt, go up into the mountains, to your father's old hunting place. There are good, fat sheep up there. After all, what kind of a meal will a sparrow make? Put away your falcon. Get a bow and some arrows, and go hunt sheep."

David went home and stood before his uncle. "Uncle, why did you never tell me that my father had hunting grounds in the mountains? You must give me a bow and some arrows and take me to the hunting place."

"Who told you about that hunting ground?" Ohan said.

"Never mind about that. Tell me where it is, and give me a bow and some arrows."

"We don't have the hunting ground anymore. When Msrah Melik and his armies came, they took it over. We don't dare go up there for fear of Melik's wrath."

David scoffed. "Melik's wrath means nothing to me. Now, get me a bow and some arrows, and get your own hunting gear. We're going up there to see what that place is like now."

Ohan protested some more, refusing to take David and refusing to give him a bow.

Finally, David said, "If you don't do as I say, I will hurt you."

At that, Ohan gave in. He went into another room and brought out a mighty bow and a quiver of arrows. "This was your father's bow, the bow of Medz Mher. No one has used it since he died because no one has been strong enough to string it. Maybe you are strong enough."

David took the bow and strung it easily. He strapped the bow and quiver to his back. "Now fetch your bow and quiver. We're leaving."

David followed his uncle up into the mountains. Soon they came across a place that once had been enclosed by a wall, but now the wall was a crumbling ruin, and the forest beyond was overgrown and ill-kept. Not one bit of game was in sight.

"What is this place?" David asked.

"This, lad, is your father's game preserve, or what is left of it since Melik took it for himself," Ohan replied.

David and his uncle spent the rest of the day exploring the abandoned reserve. When it began to get dark, they found a place to set up their camp. Ohan lay down and went to sleep immediately, but David was restless. He sat beside his snoring uncle as the light faded from the sky, wondering what he would do about his father's game preserve.

After some hours, a flickering light in the distance caught David's eye.

I wonder what that is, David thought, and without waking his uncle, he began to climb up the mountainside toward the light.

When he got to the top of the mountain, he found a slab of white marble that had been cleft in two, and from the cleft, a flame leaped up. David raced back down the mountain and roused his uncle.

"Uncle! Uncle! Wake up! There's something you need to see!" David said.

Ohan sat up, blinking blearily. "What is it that is so important that you rouse an old man from his sleep in the middle of the night?"

"Look!" David pointed up the mountain slope to where the light still flickered and danced. "I already went up there and found a marble slab that was cleft in two and a flame burning from out of the cleft."

"Ah. Yes, I know what that is. The marble slab is all that is left of the altar of the monastery that your father built, the monastery of Our Lady of Marout. Your father's tomb was in the monastery, but I expect that was damaged as well when Melik and his army invaded Sassoun. They wrecked the monastery just like they wrecked the game preserve."

"Oh, Uncle, we must rebuild it right away. We have to rebuild this monastery. Go into the town and gather up all the stonemasons and carpenters and workmen you can find. Send them here now so that we can rebuild this holy place. I will wait for you here. And when the monastery is rebuilt, you will go and gather monks and priests and bishops so that they can live here and worship God as they ought to do, and the people of Sassoun will have this holy place restored as my father would have wished it to be."

Ohan knew better than to argue when David was in this sort of mood, so he immediately set off down the mountainside and into the town. He told all the people that David intended to restore the monastery, and soon every artisan and builder and worker in stone and wood from miles around hastened up the mountain to help with the work.

Everyone worked as hard as they could and as quickly as they could, and soon the monastery was restored to its former state and peopled with holy men to sing Mass and say the other prayers they were wont to offer throughout the day. Not until the monastery was rebuilt and peopled with monks did David descend from the mountain peak.

It didn't take long for Msrah Melik to hear that the monastery had been rebuilt. "It's that infidel David who's behind this I'll wager. And I have just recalled that I've not had tribute from Sassoun for seven years now. It's high time my army paid them a visit and put them in their place."

Melik summoned the generals of his army. Their leader was a man named Gospadin.

Melik said to Gospadin, "Gather your men. Go to Sassoun. Collect up all the treasure they owe me, seven years' worth, and bring me the best of their women. We could use some more slaves. And when you're done collecting everything, raze Sassoun to the ground. Then kill that rogue David, and bring me his head."

"I will do this, but I expect to be well paid for it," Gospadin said.

"Never fear. If you manage all of that, you can have half my kingdom."

Gospadin mustered a thousand soldiers and placed his most trusted lieutenants in positions of command. Then they marched on Sassoun, relishing the thought that soon they would be wealthy and their enemy's country razed to the ground.

Gospadin and his men made their camp and sent a messenger into the town.

The messenger went to Ohan and said, "Msrah Melik has sent his army to collect the tribute you owe him, seven years' worth, and the best of your women. Gospadin, the general of the army, is on his way now. If you do not pay, the army will slaughter every last one of you and take everything anyway."

Ohan paled at the words of the messenger. "We will pay, never fear."

As soon as the messenger had gone, Ohan went in search of his nephew.

"David, my lad, it's been too long since we've eaten any game. How about you go up the mountainside and see whether you can catch a fine sheep for our dinner?" Ohan did this because he was ashamed of paying tribute to Melik and didn't want David to know about it.

David took his bow and quiver and went hunting. Not long afterward, Gospadin and his army arrived at the gates of Sassoun. The soldiers went throughout the city and the farmsteads around. They took all the cattle and goats and sheep and put them in a holding pen together. Then they chose the best of the women and locked them in a barn to wait while they collected the rest of the tribute.

Meanwhile, David was hunting in the mountains. He soon came across a fine, fat sheep, and when he had killed it, he hoisted it onto his shoulders and set off for home. On the way, he stopped at the farm owned by the old woman and pulled up a turnip to munch on his way home. When David arrived at the town, he saw the people in mourning.

The old woman caught sight of David, and with tears streaming down her cheeks, she said, "So this is what the champion of Sassoun does when our enemies come to call: He goes to my turnip field and helps himself while Msrah Melik's soldiers take everything we own. Those soldiers even took my daughter, curse you! My only daughter! And you stand by like nothing has happened at all! They've taken all the cattle, sheep, and goats, and now they're sitting in the treasure house counting out your father's gold to take back to that monster, Melik!"

"I was away hunting, Old One. Show me where they took your daughter. I will help her," David said.

The old woman showed David the barn where the women were being held. David broke down the door and set the women free. Next, David went to the place where Melik's soldiers were keeping the herds and flocks and set the animals free.

"Now, Old One, show me where they're counting out the gold," David said.

The old woman pointed to the treasure house. Outside the door, forty soldiers were standing guard.

With the sheep he had killed in the mountains slung over his shoulder, David strode up to the guards and said, "I heard that my uncle is in there and that he needs my help."

"Did you now? Well, I expect that someone was playing tricks on you. Go home, boy. You're not wanted here," the chief of the guards said.

At that, David put down the sheep and attacked the guards. He wrung the necks of every last one of them and left their bodies piled up just outside the door. Then David picked up the sheep again and went into the treasure house, where he saw his Uncle Ohan and his Uncle Vergo counting out treasure and putting it into sacks while Msrah Melik's generals looked on. Ohan was holding the sack open while Vergo scooped up gold with a bucket and poured it in. They had already filled several sacks, which had been lined up against one wall.

"Uncle Ohan! Uncle Vergo!" David said as he put down the sheep's carcass. "You really shouldn't be doing that. That's work for younger men. Let me help you."

"Get rid of this brat. Get him out of here and get on with your work," Gospadin told Ohan.

"No, I will stay and help. It is my duty to help my elders," David said.

"Go away, David. We don't want any trouble. Vergo and I can do this ourselves," Ohan told his nephew.

"No, I think I'll stay and help." David took the bucket from his uncle and held it upside down. "Now, Uncle, a measure of gold for Msrah Melik."

Ohan put a shovelful of gold onto the bottom of the upturned bucket. Then David went over to the sack, shook the gold off the bucket and onto the floor, and then pretended to empty the bucket into the sack.

"There! One scoop of treasure. See how helpful I can be?" David said.

"Get out! Get out before I slice off that fool head of yours and set the entire town ablaze!" Gospadin shouted.

In response, David hurled the bucket at Gospadin. If Gospadin hadn't ducked just in time, the bucket surely would have killed him. Gospadin became frightened and tried to run away, but David caught him, cut off his lips, pulled out his teeth, and lodged the teeth in his forehead.

Then David tied Gospadin to a horse and said, "Go back to Msrah Melik and tell him that the son of Medz Mher did this. Also tell Melik that what happened to you will happen to him if he ever tries to take tribute from us again. Our treasure, cattle, and women don't belong to him. Let him have Msr, and let us have Sassoun. But if he won't be satisfied with what he already has, let him come here so that I can deal with him."

Gospadin and the other generals raced back to their country, leaving their troops behind. But the soldiers didn't mind; they had set off on their own way to enjoy the treasure, women, and slaves they had looted from the town. It didn't take long for David to catch up to the soldiers of Msrah Melik.

"Hey, there! You're taking things that don't belong to you. That's not a very nice thing to do. Give it all back, or something bad will happen to you," David said.

The soldiers laughed. "Yes, and what are you going to do about it if we don't give it back? We're a whole army here, and you are only one man."

At that, David took his spear and fell upon the soldiers of Msrah Melik. He didn't stop fighting until he had killed every last one of them.

Then David set all the captives free and said, "Help me bring all this treasure back home so that we can give it back to whoever owns it."

The captives helped David bring everything back to Sassoun, where David ensured that the captives were returned safely to their families and every bit of treasure went only to the person it belonged to.

David's Battle with Msrah Melik

When Gospadin and the other generals returned to Msr, they were so ashamed that they hid. It wasn't until Melik asked whether his army had returned with the tribute that someone told him what had happened. Melik then summoned Gospadin to account for himself. When Gospodin arrived, Melik saw the wounds that David had inflicted upon him.

"Whatever happened to you?" Melik asked, astonished at Gospadin's appearance. "And where is the treasure? Where are the cattle and the sheep and the women?"

Gospadin fell on his face before his king. "O mighty one, long may you reign. Did you not see what happened to my face? David did this, Medz Mher's whelp. I don't know what happened to my soldiers. They went their way, and I went mine. And David has a message for you."

"Indeed. Tell it to me."

"David says that if you're not satisfied with having your own country but want his as well, you need to go to Sassoun so that he can deal with you."

When Melik heard this, he fell into a rage. "Assemble my army! Every male able to bear arms is to come here at once! I don't care how young or old, give each one a shirt of mail, a helmet, and a sword and tell him that we march on Sassoun tomorrow!"

Now, Ohan was in great fright after David sent Gospadin and the other generals running back home and after he had killed all of Melik's soldiers. Ohan knew it was only a matter of time before Melik assembled another, larger army and marched straight to Sassoun, and this time, no amount of treasure would keep him from killing everyone and burning down their homes.

So, one day, as Ohan made the rounds that he had appointed for himself—to watch for Melik's army— he saw a great host of tents had been erected on the plain not far from the town. Ohan ran back home as fast as he could and called for his nephew.

"What is it, Uncle? What frightens you so?" David asked.

"I told you! I told you your actions would be our doom! Even now, Melik's host is camped on our doorstep. There are too many tents to count. It looks like snow has fallen on the plain. There are so many white tents so close together. We are doomed. We should gather our women and our treasure and fly, right now, or we are all dead!" Ohan said.

"Never fear, Uncle. I'll keep us all safe."

David rushed over to the home of the old woman who was his friend.

"Old One, I need your help. Have you an old poker or skewer or something I can have? And can I borrow your donkey?"

"Whatever for?" the old woman asked.

"Msrah Melik has arrived with his army. They've covered the plain with their tents. I'm going to make war on them."

"Make war? The very son of Medz Mher will go to war astride a donkey with a rusty old skewer in one hand? Over my dead body, you are. Listen to me, you young fool. Your father had the best weapons in the world. He had the Lightning Sword. He had a mail shirt so tough that no weapon could pierce it and a shining helmet to go with it. He had the fiercest, fastest steed in the whole world, Kourkig Jelaly himself. You need to get those things if you want to fight Melik and the host of Msr properly, as befits the son of Medz Mher."

"Tell me where I can find them, then."

"Oh, no, that I'll not do. Your uncle put a curse on anyone who tells where those things are hidden. No, if you want to find them, you'll have to pry that information out of Ohan."

David ran home. He grabbed his uncle by the shirt and lifted him off the ground. "Tell me where I can find my father's weapons and my father's horse. Tell me now, or I'll break your neck right here."

"Put me down, and I'll bring them to you, and a curse on the one who told you this," Ohan said.

David put Ohan down. Ohan went to the place where the weapons and the horse were kept and brought them back to David. David put on the mail shirt, helmet and strapped on his father's sword. He saddled and bridled the horse and mounted it. When Ohan saw David thus arrayed for battle, he began to weep.

"Oh, alas! Alas for the mail shirt and helmet! Alas for the Lightning Sword! Alas for Kourkig Jelaly!" he cried.

When David heard this, he became very angry. He was about to get off the horse and shout at his uncle when Ohan said, "Alas for David! Alas for the champion of Sassoun! Alas for the son of Medz Mher!"

Hearing his uncle's lament, David dismounted. He took his uncle's hand in his and gently kissed it. "Don't weep for me, Uncle. You have been a father to me, and I am grateful. But don't weep. I'll be home soon. You'll see."

David rode through the town dressed in his father's armor and armed with his father's sword, riding his father's steed. All the people of Sassoun rejoiced to see their champion on his way to fight for them.

"It's like Mher himself has come back to save us!" they said and cheered and sang for David to the gates of the city.

Now, David had another uncle named Toros, a giant of a man who was his mother's brother. When Toros saw David riding out to war, he uprooted an elm tree and hoisted it onto his shoulder.

Toros went to the camp of Melik's army and shouted, "Hey, you there! You in the tents! Don't you know that you're in Sassoun and David, the son of Medz Mher, is on his way to fight you?"

Then he took the tree in both hands and swung it around so that it swept away twenty of the tents with the men still inside them.

"Hey there!" Toros shouted as he swung away with the tree. "Make way for David! Give the lad room to fight!"

David rode Kourkig Jelaly up onto a rise near the camp.

He shouted in a great voice at Melik's army. "Get up! Stand on your feet! I won't have it said that I killed you while you were abed. Put on your armor! Mount your horses! I am here to make war on Msrah Melik!"

Then David put spurs to Kourkig Jelaly and roared into Melik's camp. Up and down the camp, he rode, laying about him with his father's sword. David fought through the whole morning and past the noon hour, and not one of Melik's soldiers could stand against him.

Finally, one old man in Melik's army said, "Let me go and talk to David. Maybe I can put a stop to this slaughter."

The old man went to David and said, "Young one, I am here to talk, not fight. Will you hear me?"

"I will," David replied.

"Look about you, at all the men you have slaughtered. They are old and young. Some of them had wives at home, and some had children. All had parents and uncles and aunts, sisters and brothers, who now will be in mourning. You don't know any of the men you killed, and they don't know you. What harm has any of us done to you? We came here because Melik forced us to. He said that he would kill us if we did not put on the armor he gave us and take up a sword against Sassoun. If your quarrel is with Melik, why don't you take it to him and leave the rest of us alone?"

"Very well. Tell me where I can find Melik, and I will do as you ask."

"His tent is the big one in the middle of the camp. You can see smoke coming out of the hole at the top. But that's not the smoke of a fire. That's Melik's breath."

David spurred Kourkig Jelaly and rode to the center of the camp. He reined in his horse at the entrance to Melik's tent.

"Where is Msrah Melik? Where is he skulking, hiding away while his men fight and die for him?" he shouted.

The soldiers who stood guard outside Melik's tent replied, "Our king is within, but he is asleep. It is his custom to sleep for seven days at a time. He has only been asleep for three days. There are four yet left before he wakes."

David was astounded. "How is it that your king will lie here peacefully asleep and not fight alongside his men? Go and wake him, now, so that I can put him to sleep for good."

The soldiers went into Melik's tent. They slapped the bare feet of their king, but all he did was mutter about fleas and roll over, still dead asleep. They heated a plowshare on the fire and held the hot metal against their king's back. This time Melik muttered about mosquitos, but he also woke up enough to see David standing there at the entrance to the tent. Melik sent a great blast of breath at David, with force enough to knock over many strong men. When David did not even waver, Melik roused himself all the way. The two men locked eyes for a long moment, and as they did so, Melik felt the strength ebbing out of his body.

But wily Melik was not so easily defeated.

He sat up and said, "Welcome, David. Come and sit on that rug so that we can talk awhile."

Now, when on campaign, Melik had the habit of digging a deep pit inside his tent and covering the hole with a rug. He would lure his enemies into the tent, and when they fell through the hole, he would have it blocked up and leave his victims to rot. Melik had done the same here, so when David came into the tent and stepped onto the rug, he fell into the deep shaft that Melik had dug.

Melik looked over the lip of the pit and leered at David. "The son of Medz Mher, indeed. You shall trouble me no more, young cur. You have met your match in me and your doom."

Then Melik ordered the pit to be covered by a millstone so that David could not escape.

That night, David's Uncle Ohan tossed and turned in his sleep. Finally, his wife could stand it no longer.

"Quit thrashing about like an eel, or I'll send you to the barn to sleep in the loft," she said.

"I've been having bad dreams. I think our David is in trouble," Ohan told her.

"The only trouble here is the trouble you'll be in if you don't let me sleep."

"Curse you, woman. I'll let you sleep all right. See? I'm getting out of bed. I'm going to go and find out what happened to our David if it's the last thing I do."

"Good. You go look for that silly little beast, and in the meantime, I'll get some rest."

Ohan dressed and put on his mail shirt and girded on his sword. Then he went to the barn where his horses were stabled.

He slapped the white horse on the rump and asked it, "How fast can you get me to Melik's camp?"

"I can have you there by morning," the horse replied.

"What use is that? I'm trying to rescue that young fool David, not attend his funeral."

Ohan went and slapped the red horse on the rump and asked it, "How fast can you get me to Melik's camp?"

"I can get you there in an hour," the horse replied.

"An hour? An hour? That's how you repay me for all the fine barley I feed you?"

Ohan went and slapped the black horse on the rump and asked it, "How fast can you get me to Melik's camp?"

"If you saddle and mount me now, I'll have you there before you get your right leg over my back and into the stirrup," the horse replied.

Ohan saddled the black horse and put his left foot into the stirrup. He started to swing himself up into the saddle, but before he could find his seat, the black horse took off like a bolt of lightning, and by the time Ohan had sat down and put his right foot into the stirrup, they were already on the ridge overlooking Melik's camp.

Kourkig Jelaly saw Ohan arrive and galloped up to him, neighing. When Ohan saw David's horse, his heart fell.

Our David is dead for sure. Or if not dead, taken captive, he thought.

Now, Ohan had a nickname: Big Voice. He was called this because he could shout and roar louder than any man alive. Ohan knew that the only way to find David was to roar and that he would have to roar louder than he had ever roared before. Ohan took seven ox hides and strapped them around his body so that his ribs would not break when he roared.

When all was ready, he stood at the edge of the ridge facing the camp and shouted: "David, my David, if you can hear me, invoke Our Lady of Marout! Invoke the Holy Cross! Our Lord and Lady will give you the strength to come home to me!"

So loud was Ohan's roar that David heard it even at the bottom of the pit.

"That's my uncle!" he said, and his heart leaped. Then he said, "May Our Lady of Marout and the Holy Cross give me strength!"

Gathering himself up, he coiled like a spring and jumped. He jumped so hard that he smashed right through the millstone, and to this day, there are pieces of that stone that have yet to fall to earth.

Melik saw that David had escaped the pit. "David! How pleasant to see you again. Come, sit and talk with me a while."

"I'll not sit with you ever again, and I'll not talk. Get your weapons and meet me in fair combat. If you refuse, you'll just prove yourself a coward—as if you haven't already by the way you took me prisoner," David said.

"Very well, but I reserve the right to strike the first blow."

"All right. You can strike first. I'll meet you on the plain when you're ready."

Msrah Melik strapped on his armor, mounted his horse, and took up his lance. He rode out to the plain where he found David waiting for him.

"I get the first blow, remember?" Melik said.

"I remember. Get on with it," David replied.

Melik knew that he would need a lot of power behind his blow if he were going to win the contest, so he rode his horse all the way to Diarbarkir, and then turned around and thundered back to the place where David was standing. He charged forward and struck a blow so mighty that the people back in the town wondered whether there had been an earthquake, while in the camp, the dust was so thick that it was hard to make out the outlines of the nearest tents.

"Ha! That will be the end of that pesky David. I'm sure no one could have survived that," Melik said.

But then David said, "No, sorry, you're wrong. I'm still here," and as the dust cleared, Melik saw David standing there, unhurt.

Melik was astonished. "Oh, well, I guess I didn't get enough of a run-up, then. Can I have another go?"

"Very well."

This time, Melik rode all the way to Aleppo. He rode back to the plain so fast that the wind of his passing was like a hurricane, and when he struck David, the ground shook, and the thunder rumbled, and the lightning flashed.

"That had to have been the end of David," Melik said, who couldn't see more than a few feet in front of him for all the rain and dust his charge had stirred up.

"No, sorry, still here," David said when the dust began to clear. "Is it my turn now?"

"Not yet. Obviously, my run-up wasn't good enough that time either. Can I have one more try?"

"One more, and then I get to have a go."

This time, Melik rode all the way to Msr. He came roaring back with such force that when he struck David, a cloud of dust went up above the tops of the mountains and blotted out the sun for three whole days.

When the dust began to clear, Melik said, "There. I've finally gotten rid of David. Sassoun is mine."

"No, sorry, it's not. I'm still here, and I believe it's my turn now," David said.

When Melik heard David speak and saw him standing there unhurt, he felt as though his bones had turned to water. He ran back to his tent, dove into the pit he had dug, and commanded that the pit be covered with forty oxhides and the hides be covered with forty millstones.

But Melik could not hide from David. David mounted his horse, drew his sword, and set off toward the camp and Melik's tent. On the way, an old woman ran onto David's path and threw herself at the horse's feet.

"O David! Melik is my son. Don't kill him. Kill me instead!" the old woman cried.

"I will count this as my first blow, even though I forbear to strike," David told her.

Then he spurred his horse and again rode toward the camp.

He hadn't gone far when a young woman ran onto his path and threw herself at the horse's feet.

"O David! Melik is my brother. Don't kill him. Kill me instead!" the young woman cried.

"I will count this as my second blow, even though I forbear to strike. Now, stand aside, for I have but one blow remaining, and I must make sure it hits home," David told her.

David spurred his horse into a gallop. When they got closer to Melik's tent, they saw the forty millstones piled on top of the pit. Kourkig Jelaly made a mighty leap, and on the way back down, David struck a colossal blow with the Lightning Sword of Medz Mher. So violent was that stroke that it shattered all forty millstones, cut through the forty ox hides, and sliced Msrah Melik in half.

Kourkig Jelaly lightly touched down to earth, and David wheeled him around to see what had become of his foe.

A faint voice from the bottom of the pit said, "Sorry, I'm still here. I'm not dead yet."

David was astonished. It surely was impossible that anyone had survived such a blow. He went and peered over the edge of the pit. There he saw Msrah Melik standing tall.

"If you're really still alive, prove it. Move about a bit," David said.

Melik moved a little, and as he did so, his body fell into two halves, one half falling one way and the other half falling another. When Melik's soldiers saw this, they quaked with fear.

"Don't be afraid. My war with you is done. You are not to blame for this. You are farmers and fishermen, cobblers and carpenters, all forced to come here against your will. Go home to your families. Ply your trades. But if any of you dare come back here to threaten Sassoun, you will have me to deal with. Go home to your families. Live good lives. Be prosperous. And tell everyone in Msr what happens when tyrants threaten freeborn people," David told them.

The Knight in the Panther's Skin (*Georgia*)

"The Knight in the Panther's Skin" is an epic poem in quatrains by medieval Georgian poet Shota Rustaveli (c. 1160-after c. 1220), whose surname suggests that he was from Rustavi, a city in Southeastern Georgia. Rustaveli was Finance Minister under Queen Tamar (r. 1184-1213). His story of the trials of Tariel and Avtandil, the two knights around whom the story revolves, is considered to be the Georgian national epic; at one time, every Georgian bride was expected to have a copy of the book as part of her dowry and be able to recite portions for her husband.

The epic begins with a long prologue in which Rustaveli praises Queen Tamar (to whom he refers as "King Tamar") and sets out the philosophical underpinnings of the poem that is to follow. The story is a romance in the medieval sense of the term; it is an episodic tale of quests, knightly deeds, and romantic love. Rustaveli claims it to be his rendering of a Persian story; however, the model for Rustaveli's epic has yet to be found, assuming that such a model ever existed in the first place. That said, the knight in the panther's skin does bear some superficial resemblance to the Persian hero Rostam, in that he also wears the skin of a great cat, is nearly invincible in battle, and rides a horse as fast as lightning.

The retelling presented below has been both rendered into prose and abridged to fit this present volume. We join the story after the knight Avtandil and his liege lord, Rostevan, have encountered the strange warrior in the panther's skin. Rostevan becomes obsessed with finding the man, needing to reassure himself that the man was truly human and not a demonic apparition. When messengers sent throughout the land cannot find the man, Rostevan decides that he must have been an apparition and lets go of the matter. However, Rostevan's daughter, Tinatin, who has been made ruler of the land by her father and with whom Avtandil is deeply in love, is not convinced that her father has been completely cured of his obsession, nor does she believe that the man was an apparition.

Tinatin, who returns Avtandil's affections, therefore sends Avtandil on a three-year quest to find the stranger in the panther's skin. Avtandil's journey starts with only a single quest, but by the end, it has seen him go through a series of adventures filled with danger, battles, romantic love, and knightly courtesy.

Avtandil Meets the Knight in the Panther's Skin

Avtandil searched and searched for the mysterious knight until only three months were left to find him. He had just made camp for the knight when a party of hunters approached.

"Help us! Our brother has been struck by a madman and is dying!" the hunters said.

The men told their story to Avtandil, whose heart leaped when he heard that the madman they spoke of was none other than the knight he was seeking.

"Hey, there he goes now!" one of the hunters cried.

There across the plain, Avtandil could see the knight in his panther's skin, cantering along on a jet-black horse.

"You may stay here in my camp and eat of the game I caught. My quest is to find that man, and now I must leave," Avtandil told the hunters.

Avtandil mounted his horse and raced after the man in the panther's skin. As he rode, he thought about how best to approach the man.

"He doesn't seem to like people asking questions, and he certainly demands a great deal of respect. Maybe I should hang back and watch him for a while and then decide what to do," he said to himself.

For two days, the stranger rode on, and for two days, Avtandil followed him. On the third day, they came to a cliff. In the cliff's face was the entrance to a cave, and a stream flowed out of the cave and burbled its way through beds of rushes and stands of trees.

Here, Avtandil dismounted his horse. He climbed as high as he could into one of the trees, giving him a commanding view of the stream and forest. He watched the stranger ride by, only stopping when he reached the mouth of the cave. There he dismounted, and out of the cave came a lovely woman. The woman led the horse into the cave and took off its saddle and bridle. She helped the man remove his armor, and then both of them went into the cave together just as the sun set and night fell.

Avtandil remained watching in the tree all night long, still wondering how he might find a way to speak to the man. In the morning, the woman helped to saddle and bridle the horse and then helped the man put on his armor. The man and the woman embraced, and then the man mounted his horse and rode away, while the woman stayed behind, shedding many bitter tears.

The man in the panther's skin rode along the stream, retracing his path from the day before. On his way through the trees, he passed by the place where Avtandil had hidden. Avtandil was finally able to get a good look at the stranger and was struck by the man's beauty. Avtandil did not doubt that this man could wrestle a lion and come away the victor. At first, Avtandil thought to jump on his own horse and follow the man, but then he thought better of it.

I'll go to the cave and talk with the woman. Maybe she can tell me the strange knight's story, and maybe she can introduce us later, he thought.

Avtandil climbed down from the tree and led his horse to the mouth of the cave. No sooner had he arrived than the young woman came running out, obviously thinking that her knight had come back, but when she saw Avtandil, she turned and ran back into the cave in fright. Avtandil followed and grabbed her by the wrist.

The young woman struggled to get free, all the while crying out, "Tariel! Tariel!"

"Don't worry. I won't hurt you! I mean you no harm. I'm here to ask about the knight who just left. From what you said, I gather his name is Tariel. Can you tell me about him?" Avtandil said.

The woman stopped struggling. "I'll not tell you anything. That story is not for your ears, and even if you ask me a hundred times, I'll not speak a word of it to you."

"Please, you have no idea what I have gone through to find that man. I have to know who he is, and you have to tell me."

The woman continued to refuse, and Avtandil continued to ask, until finally, Avtandil lost all patience.

He grabbed the woman by the hair and set a knife to her throat. "Tell me who that man is, or I will kill you."

"Go ahead. You won't get his story from me while I live, and when I'm dead, I certainly won't tell you anything. I'd rather die than speak to you."

At this, Avtandil let the woman go. He sheathed his knife and sat down on a nearby stone, his eyes filled with tears.

Then he knelt before the woman and said, weeping, "I have treated you very ill and have no right to expect that you'll forgive me. But you should know that I have done everything I have done because of love. My beloved Tinatin sent me here to find out who that man is, and I would rather die than disappoint her."

The woman saw Avtandil's tears and said, "A lover's path is often cruel, and love can make a man do things he might not otherwise do. I do forgive you, but I still won't tell you the knight's story. That is for him alone to tell. At least, our names I can give you: I am Asmat, and he is Tariel. You may wait here until he returns. I'll explain to him your plight and your quest, and maybe he will tell you what you want to know."

Just then, they heard the sound of a horse's feet splashing through the stream.

"Quick, hide! It will take some time to convince him to speak with you, and no stranger who has demanded speech of him has yet lived to hear the answer," Asmat said.

Asmat showed Avtandil a place where he could hide and then went to greet Tariel. As before, she helped unsaddle the horse and take off its bridle, and then she helped the knight take off his armor. She led the knight into the cave and had him sit down on one of the panther's skins that lined the floor. Then she lit a fire and began to cook something for them to eat. The entire time, tears coursed down the knight's cheeks, and when the meal was ready, he took only a few bites before throwing himself down on the couch that lay nearby, still weeping.

"Tariel, my dearest one, it pains me to see you thus. Every day you come back, and every day, you shed bitter tears. I may not be able to cure your grief, but surely it would help to share it with a friend? What you need is a brother in arms, a fellow knight who understands you and who can help you," Asmat said.

"Asmat, dear Asmat, I know you speak true, but I doubt there is anyone in the world who could befriend me like that."

Asmat knelt next to Tariel. "If I could bring you such a man, would you promise not to hurt him?"

"Indeed, I would promise that if you could find me such a companion. But I expect my promise will go to waste. I think such a man is someone who only lives in dreams."

Asmat went to the place where Avtandil was hiding.

"Come. I think he will speak with you," she said and led Avtandil to Tariel. "Tariel, this is Avtandil. He is a knight like you, and I think he could be your friend."

Tariel sat up and looked at Avtandil, and his heart was instantly filled with love for the young knight. Likewise, Avtandil gazed upon Tariel and found that he loved him as well.

The two men embraced and shook hands, and when they had finished greeting one another, Tariel said, "Come, be seated next to the fire, and tell me your story."

"I am a knight from Arabia. My liege lord's daughter, Tinatin, is my beloved, and for her, I would die. Her father, my liege lord, and I saw you once when we were out hunting. My lord sent some men to summon you back to meet him, but you killed them all and ran away, so Tinatin has sent me on a quest to find you. She gave me three years. That span will be up in only a few months. I had despaired of finding you, but then I encountered some hunters. You had wounded one of them with your whip, and they pointed you out to me. I followed you here and spoke with Asmat. She bade me wait, and then brought me here to you."

"Ah, yes, I remember the day of which you spoke. I now rue having killed those men. I was so deep in my thoughts that I did not realize they were messengers and not soldiers sent to kill me. As for the men you met, they tried to lay hands on me for no good reason, and so I defended myself." Tariel sighed. "Alas for those who burn in the fires of love! Asmat spoke true when she said you would be a boon companion for me. You also are a knight, and you also have a beloved from whom you have been parted. I am glad you have come to me, for your friendship is a little balm for my grief."

"Tariel," Asmat said, who had been sitting nearby and listening to the men, "why don't you tell Avtandil your story? You've held it in your breast for so long. It might bring you some comfort to share it with a friend."

"As always, you are wise, dear Asmat—although I fear the telling might be the death of me, so painful is the wound I bear because of love. But you are right. I should tell Avtandil my tale," Tariel said.

"I am listening, and any aid I might give you is yours for the asking," Avtandil said.

The Knight Tells His Tale

"My father was a vassal to Parsadan, the King of India. So well-beloved was my father that when he got my mother with child, Parsadan asked whether he might foster me since he and his queen had not been able to have children of their own. My parents were honored, and accordingly, I was brought up as though I were an heir of the blood. I was given the best teaching, both for mind and body, and by the time I was five years old, I could wrestle a full-grown lion and take no hurt myself. But that fifth year also saw my undoing: The queen found herself with child, and when her time came, she delivered a daughter, who was named Nestan-Daredjan.

"There are no words to praise the beauty of Nestan-Daredjan. She was my childhood companion from the day of her birth until she reached her tenth year, and I my fifteenth. It was then that her father sent her away to be tutored, for she was now the heir to Parsadan's throne. I went back to live with my parents, and for a time, I was happy, while my beloved Nestan-Daredjan lived in a tower her father had built for her, learning everything she needed to know from Parsadan's widowed sister, and tended by dear Asmat here and one other maid.

"When my father died, Parsadan gave me his place at court. I now found myself lord of many lands and many vassals, and I tried to administer them as well as my father had. One day, Parsadan asked me to hunt some game birds and bring them to his daughter's tower. I did as he commanded. When I brought the birds to the tower, Asmat came down to take them from me, but as she did so, a curtain parted, and there I saw Nestan-Daredjan. From that moment forth, my heart was no longer my own, and I became weak with love. The king and queen fretted over me. No doctor could cure my malady, and I dared not speak my love for fear of being banished from court.

"After a time, I felt better and went about my duties and my leisure almost as usual, though my heart still burned for Nestan. Then one day, my dear Asmat came to me bearing a letter. It was from Nestan-Daredjan, and O blissful day, the letter declared that she also loved me! I wrote back, confessing my love to her, and so it was that we first spoke of our joy.

"We sent letters to one another, secretly, for many days. Then a time came when India made war with the Khatavians. I led Parsadan's army, and despite the treachery of the Khatavian king, we won the day and brought the king and many of his soldiers back to India as captives. Everyone rejoiced at my victory, and at the victory banquet, my heart nearly burst, for my beloved Nestan was there sitting beside me at the feast. We contrived to meet in person a few times after that, and both thought that our joy would soon be complete.

"Then one day, Parsadan and his queen called me and their other advisors to their council chamber. They told us they had been considering marriage for their daughter and wanted to hear our opinions. I could hardly breathe. Would I soon have my heart's desire? No, that was not to be, for they were thinking to marry her to the son of the king of Khvarazm. What could I do but agree? Soon the matter was settled, and the sun was made dark in my eyes.

"The next day, my beloved summoned me. She accused me of treachery, of conspiring to marry her to someone else. I told her that the decision had been made without me, and her anger cooled.

Then she said, 'If you love me, you will do something for me.'

'Anything,' I said.

'You will kill my bridegroom.'

I agreed to do it.

"When the wedding party arrived, they set up tents and pavilions outside the city. That night, I crept into the bridegroom's tent. I beheaded him and stuck his head on a pole. Then I fled, accompanied by my most loyal followers. Parsadan soon found out what I had done and sent a letter to me.

'Why did you bring such dishonor upon our house? If you had wanted our daughter for your own bride, you had but to ask.'

I wrote back saying that I no longer wanted his daughter and that although I was in exile because of the shame of my deed, in time, the throne of India would be mine, for who else did Parsadan have to succeed him?

"I took up residence in a fortress not far from the capital, chafing daily for news of my beloved. News I did not get until one day, I looked over the parapet and saw two travelers coming down the road. One I recognized as Asmat, but she was in a sorry state. Her hair was matted, her clothes were torn, and there was blood on her face. I rushed down to greet her and escort her to safety. When I asked her how our dear Nestan fared, she began to weep. She told me that Nestan's aunt feared that Parsadan would blame her for the plot to kill the son of the king of Khvarazm. The aunt beat Asmat and Nestan and then summoned two demons carrying a chest between them. The demons seized Nestan, put her in the chest, locked it, and then ran away—who knows where? And no one has seen Nestan since, but for one man, and even he knows not where she is.

"Asmat and I went looking for Nestan. We searched for a year, but nowhere did we find her. For a time, we resided with Nureddin Pridon, the king of a far country. He was the man who once thought he had seen Nestan. We searched and searched, but we did not find her in Pridon's land, either. Our grief led us here, and we have lived in this cave ever since. Asmat stays here and tends the hearth while I roam the world, hunting for our food, insensible to man and beast alike, seeing nothing since my sun has been taken from me.

Now you have heard all my tale, and now you should leave. Go back to your Tinatin. Lovers never should be parted."

Avtandil was silent for a time after Tariel finished his story, and when he spoke, his voice was thick with tears.

"My friend, I mourn with you for the loss of your dear Nestan. The burden you bear is so much heavier than mine. I think my back would have broken with it long since had I been in your place. But hear me: Perhaps I can bring an end to your grief. I will return to Tinatin, but I will not stay. I will beg leave to go look for your Nestan, and when I have found her, I will bring her to you, and you will have joy again."

"Dearest Avtandil," Tariel said, his tears bursting forth anew, "I bless the day when God sent you to us. Asmat said you would be a friend to me and a truer friend I could never ask for. Go with my blessing, and may someday you will return my sun to me. I hope that when that day comes, Nestan and Asmat and I may sit and feast with you and your Tinatin, and then our joy will be complete."

Avtandil Returns Home

The next day, Avtandil bid farewell to Tariel and Asmat and rode home. At Rostevan's court, he was received with music and dancing, and a great feast was prepared. At the feast, Avtandil was reunited with his beloved Tinatin, and everyone was happy.

When everyone had eaten and drunk their fill, Rostevan asked Avtandil to tell his story. Avtandil rose and told of all the adventures he had while seeking Tariel, and then he told the story of finding Tariel himself. Next, he told Tariel's story, and everyone wept when Avtandil spoke of Tariel's grief. Everyone praised Avtandil for his strength and courage, but Avtandil, still thinking of his friend's sadness, gave no answer.

After the feast, Tinatin summoned Avtandil to her private quarters. The lovers greeted one another with great joy, and then Tinatin showed Avtandil to a seat.

Tinatin then asked, "I mourn with you for Tariel's loss. Is there nothing we can do to assuage his sorrow?"

"Only one thing . . . The return of his dear Nestan-Daredjan. I told him I would go and seek her on his behalf. I promised him I would, and I need to keep my word."

"Yes, you must keep your word. I would expect nothing less from you, though my own heart will be darkened until the day you return."

Avtandil spent many days at Rostevan's court. He went hunting with the king and enjoyed banquet after banquet. Rostevan was deeply content that the knight he loved, like his own son, had returned to him. Avtandil saw this and realized that Rostevan was unlikely to grant him leave to seek Nestan, but he knew that he would go on that quest, whether he had leave or not.

After a few more days at court, Avtandil went to the king's vizier and said, "Wise One, I have a quest I must undertake. You heard me tell the story of Tariel's woe. I promised him that I would return and then go and seek his beloved. I need you to go to King Rostevan and ask his leave on my behalf."

"It's a fool who will undertake an errand he knows will get him killed, and that's exactly what Rostevan will do to me if I tell him you want to leave," the vizier said.

"Yes, that might happen, but it might not. Ask him, and I will reward you greatly."

The vizier accordingly went to Rostevan. "O most majestic of kings. I come to you with a request from the knight Avtandil. As you know, he found the knight Tariel, and he told us all of Tariel's grief. Avtandil, therefore, begs your majesty's leave to go on a quest to find the fair Nestan-Daredjan."

At this, Rostevan flew into a rage. "What? That ungrateful whelp goes away for three whole years, and when he finally comes back to the only home he's known, he wants to go away again? Of course I'll not grant him leave, and if I didn't know that he had sent you here to ask on his behalf, I'd slice your head off on the spot. Now get out of my sight!"

The trembling vizier returned to Avtandil and told him what Rostevan's reply had been. Avtandil rewarded the vizier richly, as he had promised. Avtandil then sat down and wrote a letter to Rostevan:

> *To the mighty Rostevan, King of All Araby, from his humble servant Avtandil, greetings. Fate and love both command me to do what they bid, and I pray that you will be able to forgive my disobedience. I promised my friend that I would help him find his beloved, and my love for my friend is such that I cannot bear to forsake him. I humbly beseech you that if this quest should end with my death, take all my treasure and distribute part of it to those most in need, and use the residue for the building of some noble works, like bridges or homes, from which all might benefit. I also beg of you to favor my loyal servant Shermadin, by whose hand you receive this letter. He is the wisest man I know besides yourself; take him into your service, and you will be blessed with his good counsel and faithful administration of all his duties. For yourself, I wish long life, prosperity, and victory in all your battles, and I remain, as ever, your humble servant*
>
> *Avtandil*

Avtandil gave the letter to Shermadin, with instructions to deliver it discreetly to Rostevan. Then Avtandil and Shermadin embraced, weeping many tears, for they knew they might never see one another again. Avtandil mounted his horse and rode quietly out of the gate and away from the palace.

When Rostevan heard that Avtandil had left, his grief was inconsolable.

"Avtandil was like a son to me. How shall I ever ride to the hunt again or feast at a banquet without him by my side?" he said.

He ordered the whole court to go into mourning, feeling betrayed that Avtandil had ridden away without saying farewell. Shermadin then deemed it safe to give Avtandil's letter to the king.

"Your royal majesty, I found this in my master Avtandil's chamber this morning. It is addressed to your majesty, and I expect it is his farewell to you."

Rostvan read the letter and wept more bitter tears, but his wounded heart was soothed somewhat, knowing that Avtandil had thought of him even as he was leaving disobediently.

"Let us all pray for brave Avtandil. Day and night, we will beseech the good God above to protect him, to bring his quest to a successful end, and bring him home safe to us," Rostevan said to his courtiers.

Avtandil Returns to Tariel and Asmat

Avtandil rode day and night toward the cave where Tariel and Asmat lived. When he arrived, Asmat came running out to greet him, but Avtandil could see that all was not well. Asmat looked pale and drawn, and she had been crying.

"O my sister, what has happened that you are so distraught?" Avtandil asked after they had embraced.

Asmat drew a shuddering breath. "Tariel is missing. He went out the day after you left us, and he has not been back since. I've searched for him myself, but how much can one woman do when she has not a mount to carry her?"

"Dear Asmat, have no fear. I'll look for him myself and bring him home safe. Have rugs and cushions laid and a fire burning, and wine in the cup ready for our return. I'll not be long. Keep in good heart!"

Avtandil mounted his horse and set off in the direction that Asmat had last seen Tariel go. He rode tirelessly throughout the day, his eyes always searching for his friend. The day had nearly ended when he spied Tariel's horse standing near a bed of reeds along a river. The horse's head was bowed down toward the ground, but Tariel himself was nowhere to be seen. Avtandil dismounted near Tariel's horse and went looking through the reeds. There, he found his friend, sitting near the riverbank.

"How now, dear friend. What are you doing here by yourself? Our sister Asmat mourns in your absence. Let us go home to her," Avtandil said.

Tariel didn't reply. He didn't even look up. Avtandil knelt beside him and saw that his friend was deathly pale, with sunken cheeks and matted hair, and tears were coursing down his face.

Avtandil gently wiped away Tariel's tears with his sleeve and said, "Tariel, it is I, Avtandil. I've returned as I said I would. Let's go home to Asmat. She is waiting for us."

Tariel spoke without looking at Avtandil. "Leave me alone. Leave me here and let me die. Death is all that is left for me now."

"Come now. Every lover suffers when his beloved is absent. My own heart is rent that I have had to part yet again from my dear Tinatin. What will Nestan-Daredjan do if she finds you have not the will to live, even for her? Mount your horse. Let's go home, where our sister Asmat waits for us."

Avtandil helped his friend rise and mount his horse, and together they rode back to the cave. Avtandil was pleased to see that Tariel seemed a little better for being on his horse, but he still was shocked and grieved by how ill Tariel seemed to be.

When they arrived at the cave, they found Asmat waiting for them. They dismounted, and the three friends embraced one another joyfully.

"I bless the day Avtandil became our friend, for without him, how would you have ever come home to me? Come inside, rest yourselves. We'll eat together and share our news," Asmat said.

The three went into the cave. Avtandil and Asmat helped Tariel sit on the panther's skin that Asmat always kept ready for him. Then Asmat cooked a meal, and the three talked of whatever pleased them. Asmat and Avtandil ate their fill, but Tariel barely took a bite.

When the meal was done, Tariel said, "Avtandil, my friend, it is clear that you are the most loyal of knights. You kept your promise to me and came back. But my grief is not yours to assuage. You should go back home to your beloved."

"That I'll not do. You are my brother, and I'll not see you wither away with grief. I promised to come back, and I promised to find your Nestan. How could I face my own beloved Tinatin, knowing that I turned my back on this quest? Be of good heart! Continue to live! I will go on this adventure, and if I have not returned by one year from today, you will know that I am dead, and then you may do with your life as you please," Avtandil said.

"Very well. I'll do as you ask. But I don't know what I'll do if, at the end of that year, I have neither you nor Nestan-Daredjan by my side."

In the morning, Avtandil bade farewell to Asmat.

"Come back to us soon. We need our brother here beside us," Asmat told Avtandil. Then she embraced Tariel and said, "Do not tarry. We will wait here together until Avtandil returns."

Tariel and Avtandil mounted their horses and rode away from the cave. Tariel went with Avtandil to show him what road to take to get to Pridon's land and because he was not yet ready to say farewell to his brother in arms. They rode all day, and when it came time for them to make their camp, they shot some game and roasted it over the fire.

In the morning, Tariel said, "Here we must part. Asmat awaits me. Take that road there eastward, and when you come to the seashore, ride along the beach until you come to Pridon's land. If he asks after me, you may tell him what you know."

Then the two friends embraced and said their farewells with many tears. Tariel mounted his horse and turned for home, while Avtandil mounted and rode eastward, as Tariel had told him to do.

Avtandil Visits Pridon

Avtandil rode until he came to the seashore. Then he turned his mount to ride along the coast. He traveled for seventy days, and on the seventieth day, he saw sails on the horizon. Since the ship was heading his way, Avtandil decided to wait and ask the sailors where he was and how much further he had to go.

Soon the little vessel was within shouting distance, so Avtandil called out, "Ahoy there! Can you tell me what land this is and who is its king?"

"You are standing on Turkish ground, but you are near the border with Pridon's land. Pridon is our king, the King of Mulghazanzar," the sailors replied.

"Good fortune is mine that I met you, for I ride in search of your king. Can you tell me how to find him?"

"Keep following the coastline. Two or three days' journey should bring you to the city where Pridon resides."

"Many thanks, friends, and may you always have calm seas and prosperous journeys!"

Avtandil rode on, following the coast as the sailors had told him to do. After two days, he came upon a line of men who had clearly been stationed to enclose something or someone in the field just above the beach. Avtandil spurred his horse to trot in their direction, and when he got closer, he saw that a hunting party was assembled in the field, shooting game with bows. A huge eagle flew above the party; Avtandil drew his bow and shot the eagle, which fell at the hunters' feet. The hunters turned to see who had made the shot and saw Avtandil there on his horse.

"A fine shot," one of the hunters said, but none of them dared stand in Avtandil's way; his nobility of bearing showed them that they should give him deference. Some of them even followed in his train.

On a knoll above the beach was a circle of soldiers surrounding a group of nobles, and among them was King Pridon. Pridon saw Avtandil approaching, with some of his men following along, and he said, "Go and see who that is, and find out why those men have left their stations."

The messenger ran to Avtandil and bowed before him. So stricken was he by Avtandil's beauty that he forgot what the king had told him to say.

Avtandil knew what the messenger's business was even without speech, so he said, "I am here to beg an audience of King Pridon. I am a friend to the knight Tariel, who also is known to your liege lord."

The messenger ran back to Pridon and delivered Avtandil's message. When Pridon heard Tariel's name spoken, he forgot his anger and went to greet Avtandil.

"Well met indeed. If you are a friend to Tariel, you are a friend to me. Come, ride with me to my palace, and on the way, pray tell me news of Tariel, for I have heard nothing for many a year," Pridon said.

"As your majesty pleases," Avtandil said.

All the way back to the palace, Avtandil rode beside Pridon and told him his tale—of his quest to find Tariel and how he and Tariel became brothers. Then he told Pridon of his quest to find Nestan-Daredjan. Pridon listened gladly, for he loved Tariel well and had longed to hear news of him. That night, Pridon caused a great banquet to be held in Avtandil's honor, and all who beheld the knight were awed by his beauty and courtesy. Although Avtandil was eager to resume his journey, he remained as Pridon's guest for some days, going hunting with his host and participating in the life of the court.

Finally, he went to Pridon and said, "Your majesty's gracious hospitality is matchless, but I find that I must resume my quest, for I promised Tariel I would look for Nestan-Daredjan and return within the year."

"Yes, I knew that you would soon depart, though it saddens me to see you leave. But I can't let you go without some gifts. I'll send some of my men along with you. I'll arm them well, and every last man will have a horse to ride. I'll also give you a mule to carry your provisions. I'll ride with you for a mile or two and show you the way you must go," Pridon said.

In the morning, Pridon summoned four of his best soldiers. He gave each of them new armor, new weapons, and a fierce warhorse to ride. He also gave new armor to Avtandil. The mule was duly laden with provisions, and when all was ready, Avtandil and Pridon rode out of the city together.

When they arrived at the seashore, they halted.

"This very spot is where I last saw Nestan-Daredjan. Two men were sailing her toward the shore in a small boat. It was clear to me that she was a prisoner. I drew my sword and tried to ride to her rescue, but when the men saw me, they turned their boat and fled. That was the last I saw of any of them," Pridon said.

Then Avtandil and Pridon said their farewells, and the king rode back to his court with a heavy heart, for he had come to love the young knight.

Avtandil and Patman

Avtandil and his companions rode along the seashore until they fell in with a company of merchants. They sailed with the merchants to the city of Gulansharo, and Avtandil earned the merchants' eternal friendship and praise by saving them from a band of pirates. Avtandil also decided that it might be best to disguise his true estate; if the jailers of Nestan-Daredjan were near, it would not do to let them know that a brave knight was on his way to rescue her. So, Avtandil and his companions dressed themselves like merchants and pretended to be part of the merchant band.

When the ship had been moored at the dock and the goods unloaded, Avtandil sat among the merchants, making bargains and taking orders from the servants who had been sent to buy goods for their employers. By and by, a man approached Avtandil.

Stricken by Avtandil's beauty, the man said, "Who are you and where are you from? I meet all the merchants who dock here, but I've never seen you before."

"I am a simple merchant, like all the others. But tell me of yourself. Who do you work for? What is this city? Who rules here? What do merchants customarily do when they arrive?" Avtandil replied.

"This is the city of Gulansharo. Melik Surkhavi, the King of the Sea, is our ruler. I am the gardener to Usen, the chief merchant of the city. Most merchants set aside the very best of their merchandise for Melik Surkhavi, but they first have to show that and everything else to Usen, and they have to give him gifts. Otherwise, he will ban them from trading. Would you like to meet him? I know his wife, Patman Khatun, is at home, and she always likes to meet new people. Also, you and your companions seem to have many costly wares. Usen and Patman will be grateful if you give them first pick."

Avtandil agreed that a visit to Usen and Patman would be worthwhile, so the gardener rushed home to make arrangements while Avtandil told his companions to get ready to go to their hosts' home.

When Patman heard that an exceedingly handsome merchant had arrived with costly wares, she sent ten servants to help Avtandil and his companions bring their things to the place where she lived, and while she waited for the merchants to arrive, she had her other servants set up tents for the merchants to dwell in and arranged for storage for their goods. Patman was waiting at the door for Avtandil and the other merchants. She made them very welcome while the servants tended to the pack animals and made sure the goods were all safely stored away.

In the morning, Avtandil had the merchants sent the best of their goods to the king, and after that, they began trading. Patman watched Avtandil all day and found that she desired him. She wrestled with her desire until finally, she wrote him a letter confessing her love. Avtandil received the letter and pondered what to do about it.

I do not return her affections, but she might be useful to me, and I could use her love as a lever to help find Nestan-Daredjan, he thought.

Therefore, Avtandil wrote back saying that he desired Patman in return and suggested that they meet in secret sometime soon.

After some days, Patman invited Avtandil to visit her in her chamber. Avtandil went, and they sat together on Patman's couch. Soon they progressed from sweet words to kissing, and while they were thus pleasantly engaged, a young knight burst into the room.

"And whatever is this, now?" the knight asked.

"Alas, I am undone! I am undone, and my husband and children with me!" Patman said.

"Yes, you are undone, and in the morning, I will kill your children and feed them to you, bite by bite." Then the knight left.

Patman lay weeping bitterly on her couch while Avtandil looked at her in confusion.

"Who was that man?" he asked.

"I can't tell you that. It would only make things worse. Suffice it to say that I am a woman and that I enjoy the company of men. But if you truly care about me, you'll kill that man before the night is over and bring me his ring as proof. I gave him that ring, so I'll know whether you're telling the truth," Patman replied.

"Very well, but I'll need a guide to the place where he lives."

Patman arranged for one of her servants to show Avtandil to the knight's house. When they arrived, they found the knight asleep on a couch on a terrace. Avtandil climbed silently up to the terrace, where he found two guards standing watch. He slew both before either could give the alarm. Then he went over to the young man and slit his throat. When the man was dead, Avtandil cut the ring off his finger and then tossed the body out the window and into the waves that lapped against the city's wall. Avtandil returned to Patman with the ring.

"He is dead. Here is his ring as proof. Now tell me: Who is that man, and what does he have against you? Why are you so afraid of him?" Avtandil said.

Patman's Tale

"You have saved me, and by doing so have saved my whole family. I owe you a debt, so I will tell you everything," Patman said.

"This started one night when I looked out my window and saw a small boat approaching. The boat was manned by two men, and the cargo was a large chest. When they had beached their boat, they picked up the chest, carried it up the beach, and opened it. Out of the chest stepped the most beautiful maiden I have ever seen. None can compare to her. I could see at once that the two men were brigands who had captured her. I sent some servants down to the beach to see whether they might purchase the woman's freedom. I told them that if the men refused to sell, kill them and bring the woman to me anyway.

"My servants went down to the beach while I watched from the window. For a little while, my servants haggled with the men, but when it became clear the men would never sell, I shouted, 'Kill them!' My servants beheaded the men and tossed their heads and bodies into the sea, then conducted the young woman to my house.

"I made the young woman very welcome. I asked her for her name and where she was from, and why the pirates had kidnapped her, but no matter how I asked or how often, she refused to answer. I gave her fresh clothes and put her in an apartment of my home with a servant to wait on her. I saw that she lacked for nothing. Every day I called on her to see how she was faring. Every day I asked her for her name and to tell me her tale, and every day, I got nothing but silence and tears in reply, though I could see by her clothing that she was of noble stock.

"Many days went by. I wondered how my husband would respond if he knew I was harboring this stranger. Finally, I decided that truth was better than deception, so I told Usen about the young woman. I made him promise never to tell anyone, and then I brought him to the woman's chamber. Usen was amazed by her beauty. We both sat with the woman for a while, asking her again who she was, but all she would do is weep. We wept with her—how could one not mourn with someone as beautiful and bereft as she? But even that would not soften her resolve.

"More time went by. Usen came to me and said, 'It's high time I visited the king and brought him gifts. He'll think me remiss if I don't go soon.'

"I replied, 'Very well, do as you must. But don't drink too much, and above all, don't mention our young guest to anyone!'

"Usen swore his lips were sealed, but, of course, as soon as he arrived at the banquet, he began drinking, and it didn't take long before he was in his cups. The king praised Usen for the jewels and pearls he had brought, and then Usen said, 'Aha, but I have one pearl yet that is greater than all of these,' and he told all about the young woman lodged in our home.

"The king, of course, demanded we bring our young guest to his court, and how could we refuse? I went to our guest's chamber and told her the unhappy news. 'Alas, it is my fate to be taken hither and thither. Never shall I have rest,' she said. Her grief smote my heart anew. I went to our treasure-room and chose the best jewels and pearls. I helped her hide them in her clothes. 'These may be useful to you sometime, and I'll not let a guest leave my home without a gift,' I said.

"We draped our guest in a veil, as is fitting, and brought her before the king. She received a fine welcome by his majesty and all the court, and for a time, none could speak but only gazed at her beauty. Finally, the king motioned for her to sit beside him. He asked her for her name and where she was from, but she remained steadfastly silent. Then the king thought that perhaps his son might be the one to assuage her grief. The crown prince is a good man, valiant and strong, and any woman would be proud to be his wife, but the news that the king sought to marry her to his son only refreshed the young woman's grief. Therefore, she conspired with the servants the king had given her. She gave them all her jewels and pearls, saying, 'These are yours if you help me escape.' The servants could not resist such a bribe. They clothed the woman like a servant, whisked her out of the palace, and brought her to my door.

"'Servants helped me escape the palace, but now you must help me escape this city. Have you a swift horse that can carry me a far distance?' she said.

"I could not refuse her request. I gave her our best horse, and she rode it out of the city, unseen. I shall tell you what happened to her soon, but first, I must explain who that man was, of whom I was so afraid. He was a wine taster at the king's court, handsome and well made in his body. My husband is ugly and scrawny. I did a wife's duty to Usen, but I did not desire him, and after his treachery, I cannot bear even to look at him. The wine taster I desired, and he desired me. During one fateful night of pleasure, I told the wine taster that I had helped the young woman escape, and by this, he held me in thrall, knowing that I would be doomed should he but open his lips. You cannot know what a harsh fate you have delivered me from by killing that man!"

"Men such as that deserve death. I am glad your fear is eased. Now, tell me, what happened to the young woman after she departed your house?" Avtandil said.

"I fretted daily about my young friend, wondering whether she had found succor and safety. I heard nothing of her until one day, I sat by a window that overlooked the street, and across the street was an inn. Three wayfarers came to the inn, bought food and drink, and then sat outside to eat and enjoy one another's company. They began telling their tales to one another. I listened, thinking how merry it is to hear such things, when one of the wayfarers said, 'You've all told fine tales, but I'll wager you'll think mine the best. I used to be a slave to the king of the Kadjis. When he died, his sister Dulardukht took the throne because the royal children were too young to rule. A time came when Dulardukht's sister also died, so she left for the funeral. The foreman of the slaves, a man named Roshak, said, 'Now is our chance to escape and make our fortunes. Who will come with me?'

"'Of course, we all jumped at the chance to escape servitude and seek riches. We became bandits, harassing and looting caravans as often as we could. One night we were crossing a wide plain when in the distance, we saw a light. We wondered what it was, and when it drew close enough, we saw that it was a woman and that her beauty caused the radiance. We took her to Roshak, who asked her many questions, but no answer would she give except, 'Take me to Kadjeti. I have a message for the queen.' We agreed to take her. When we arrived at the border, I begged Roshak's leave to go to Gulansharo to do some business. He assented, and so here I am, and that's all my tale.'"

"I sent one of my servants to bring the wayfarer to me. I had him tell his tale over again, and when I was satisfied I had heard all, I paid him for his trouble and sent him away. Then I summoned two of my servants, sorcerers both. I sent them to Kadjeti to see what news they might gather of she who had been my guest. They learned that Dulardukht planned to marry the young woman to her nephew and that she was being kept in a tower at the center of the city, under constant guard. The tower is encircled by three walls, one within the other, and each wall is guarded by three thousand soldiers. I don't know how she will ever escape."

"Patman, I am grateful for your tale, but I beg to know one thing: I thought Kadjis were of demon-kind, not mortal people. How is it that human beings people Kadjeti?" Avtandil said.

"They are not true Kadjis but are called such because they are great sorcerers and command mighty magic."

Upon hearing all of Patman's tale, Avtandil's heart swelled with joy near to bursting. Now that he knew where Nestan-Daredjan was, he could tell Tariel that his beloved still lived, and together they could rescue her and bring her home to her knight.

Patman, for her part, rejoiced that her heart had been unburdened of its secrets, and so she and Avtandil passed the night together in pleasure, though Avtandil held no true love for Patman and thought only of his own beloved Tinatin.

The Rescue of Nestan-Daredjan

In the morning, Patman set a meal for the two of them while Avtandil changed his clothing.

It is time I revealed my true self to my hostess, he thought, and so he set aside his merchant's garb and dressed in a manner befitting a knight.

When Patman saw him, her breath was taken away. "That look is more befitting to you than the other."

Avtandil sat next to her and said gently, "Patman, I have not told you the truth about who I am. I am not a merchant. I am a vassal of King Rostevan. I command many men and own many lands. You have been the best of friends, and you cannot know how much that means to me. But you should also know that Rostevan has a daughter who is the sun in my sky. It is because of her that I am here, and my quest is to find that young woman who you aided and is so dear to you."

Then Avtandil told all of Tariel's tale to Patman, and when he was done, he said, "And so now you know the truth. Help me to find Nestan-Daredjan and bring her to safety, back to the man she loves and who loves her more than life itself. Send one of your sorcerers to Nestan. Let her know what we intend, and so bring her some solace."

"Anything within my power to do I will do for her, and for you," Patman said.

She then wrote a letter to Nestan, explaining who Avtandil was and what he intended to do, and gave it to one of her sorcerers. "Take this to the maid in the tower in Kadjeti. Do it secretly. If she wishes to send an answer, wait for her to write it, then bring it back to me right away."

The sorcerer hastened to Kadjeti and delivered Patman's message. Nestan was wary at first, but when the sorcerer had told all his tale, Nestan understood he was a friend. She wrote a letter to Patman in answer, and the sorcerer faithfully delivered it. Patman was overcome with joy when she received the letter and read it aloud so that Avtandil could hear:

> *Dearest Patman, to receive a letter from one who is like a mother to me is the greatest joy I have had in a long while. Even though the queen of the Kadjis and her chief sorcerers are still absent, the tower where I am imprisoned is nigh unassailable! Tell those bravest of the brave that they must not make the attempt, for I would die if they were slain; I can only live knowing that my sun still shines, albeit not for me. I here enclose a letter to my Tariel. Send with it this piece of the veil he gave me so that he will know that it is truly I who wrote it. Farewell.*

When Avtandil heard Nestan-Daredjan's words, his heart was set aflame. "Patman, I must not tarry. I have to get this to Tariel and bring him back here before the queen of Kadjeti returns, for our task will be all the harder if we must face sorcerers in addition to soldiers."

"I know and understand, though my lover's heart quakes in fear for your safety. Go now and rescue the one beloved of me and your Tariel," Patman said.

Avtandil first penned a letter to Pridon, saying that Nestan-Daredjan had been found and he was going to fetch Tariel before attempting a rescue. He also asked for Pridon's aid, knowing that Pridon was a mighty warrior and had many fine soldiers at his command. He gave the letter to the servants Pridon had lent him and sent them back home with instructions to immediately give Pridon the letter.

It then was time for him to take his leave of Patman and her family. Many tears were shed, for Avtandil had become beloved of them all. Avtandil went down to the seaside and found a ship that would take him from Gulansharo to his own country by the swiftest route. When he disembarked, he rode as swiftly as he could to Tariel's cave.

First, I'll check by the river. Tariel likes to go there when he's sad. He's probably there rather than at home, Avtandil thought.

Avtandil was right; he found his friend standing amid the rushes near the river, a bloody sword in his hand, and next to him, the carcass of a lion he had slain. Avtandil jumped down from his horse and shouted a greeting to his friend. Tariel cried out with joy, and the two brothers ran to one another's arms. They embraced and kissed, delighted to see one another.

"Tariel, I have the best of news," Avtandil said.

"The best news is that you are here with me. Please don't tease me with false hopes."

"These hopes are not false. Look! I bear a letter to you, written by the hand of your beloved Nestan-Daredjan herself!"

Tariel took the letter and the scrap of veil with trembling hands. He pressed them to his lips, but when he inhaled the scent of his beloved's perfume, he fell to the ground, senseless.

"Oh, what have I done!" Avtandil cried.

He rushed to his friend's aid, but he could find neither a heartbeat nor a puff of breath. Avtandil called his friend's name, held his hand, but all to no avail. He went to the river to get some water but then thought of a better cure. He took some of the lion's blood and sprinkled it on his friend. Tariel took a breath again, and his pallor receded. He opened his eyes and found the strength to sit up. He opened Nestan's letter and read it, tears coursing down his cheeks all the while.

When he finished reading, he wiped his eyes and said, "Now is not the time for tears. It is the time for joy and laughter and knightly deeds. Come, let us go back home. We will tell Asmat the good news and arm ourselves for the coming battle. Avtandil, how can I ever repay you? The service you have rendered is worth more than my life itself. I have wept for so long, but you have dried my tears, and a new fire is rekindled in my breast."

The two friends mounted their horses and rode back to the cave, laughing and singing all the while. Asmat heard their voices and ran to greet her beloved brothers. Tears coursed down her cheeks, but these were tears of joy, not sorrow.

Tariel jumped down from his horse and ran to Asmat. "Asmat, dear Asmat! Our lives are renewed! Our brother has found our lost one!"

"Is it true? Nestan-Daredjan is found?" Asmat asked.

Avtandil alit from his horse and embraced Asmat. "It is true, dear sister! We have found her!" He showed Asmat Nestan's letter.

"Oh, this cannot be! This is not to be believed!" Asmat said.

"It is absolutely true."

Tariel then told Asmat how Nestan had been found. Tariel finished his tale, and then all three friends embraced once more.

"Come. Let's go and look at the treasure this cave holds. When I wrested it from the evil devs who lived here, I didn't care to count it, but perhaps there are things among the treasure that we might find useful in the task to come," Tariel said.

Asmat and Avtandil followed Tariel to a chamber deep within the cave. In that chamber was piled wealth immeasurable: Heaps of gold and silver as tall as a man, chests full of cut gems and pearls, embroidered silks encrusted with jewels, swords and spears, and three suits of armor, fit for a king, that no blade or bolt could pierce. Tariel and Avtandil put on some of the armor, setting aside the third suit to take to Pridon as a gift. They each took some gold and pearls, and then they sealed the treasure chamber up tight.

In the morning, the three friends started on their journey. They used some of their gold to buy a horse for Asmat, and together they rode to Pridon's country, with Avtandil as their guide. When they approached the border of Pridon's land, they saw a herd of horses with their guardian in a meadow.

"Let's play a trick on Pridon. Let's pretend to be rustlers, and when he comes storming out to see who is making off with his horses, he'll get a surprise!" Tariel said.

Avtandil and Tariel put on their armor and spurred their horses into Pridon's herd. Steed after steed, they roped and took away.

The herdsmen ran after them in vain, crying, "For shame! This is not a knightly deed, to behave as common thieves!"

One of the herdsmen set a great bonfire alight. When Pridon saw the signal fire, he armed himself and rode to the meadow with all speed. Now, Avtandil and Tariel had kept the visors of their helmets down; Pridon could not tell who they were by their dress.

Sword drawn, the king rode up to the two knights and said, "How now, what do you think you're doing with my horses?"

"Playing a trick on an old and very dear friend," Tariel replied as he lifted his visor and flashed a beaming smile at Pridon.

Then Avtandil did the same.

"God bless the two of you for knaves. And welcome, most welcome, dear friends! What took you so long? I expected your return some days ago. Come, let's go to my palace, and you can tell me all your tale. Any aid I can offer is yours for the asking," Pridon said.

Pridon had a meal set out for himself and his guests. He listened as Avtandil told him of his adventures and their plan to rescue Nestan. Then Tariel presented Pridon with the armor they had brought from the cave and the many jewels and pearls.

Pridon was overcome. "My dear friends, what have I done to deserve such largesse? Stay here and be my guests. Everything I have is yours."

Pridon had his guests conducted to fine chambers and had hot baths drawn and fresh clothing laid out for them. When Tariel and Avtandil were refreshed, they gathered with Pridon once again for a meal and to take counsel about what was to be done to free Nestan.

"If you take my advice, you'll not travel with a great host. No, three hundred of the best picked men will be more effective. We need speed if we are to get to Kadjeti before the queen and her sorcerers return," Pridon said.

Tariel and Avtandil agreed that this was the best path to follow. Pridon set preparations in motion, and in the morning, Pridon, Tariel, and Avtandil were armed and ready to ride with three hundred of Pridon's best soldiers, every man a hero. The three knights took their leave of Asmat and rode to the seashore, where they took ship to Gulansharo.

When they disembarked, Pridon said, "We should travel by night and rest by day. We need stealth now as much as we need speed."

After two nights of travel, they came within sight of the Kadji city. Its walls were massive, guarded by thousands of soldiers, and in the center rose the rock upon which Nestan's tower had been built. Tariel, Avtandil, and Pridon took counsel together about how best to assail the city and rescue Nestan. Each had a bold plan in mind, but in the end, Tariel's plan was the one they chose. Each man took with him a hundred soldiers, and each approached the city from a different side. It did not matter that they were badly outnumbered; each man fought with the ferocity of a hundred men, and none fought more fiercely than Tariel.

Avtandil and Pridon fought their way to the foot of the tower. Dead and dying guards lay everywhere, their armor rent, their blood flowing over the stones.

"Where is Tariel?" Avtandil asked.

Pridon pointed at the shattered tower door as an answer. "He is already inside. Only Tariel could have opened the door like that."

The two companions went inside and climbed the stairs, alert for enemies, but found none. When they got to the top of the stairs, there they found Tariel and Nestan-Daredjan, entwined in a long embrace. Tariel realized that they were not alone. He looked at his two companions and beamed.

"Look, my friends! The sun has returned to my day!" Tariel introduced his friends to Nestan-Daredjan.

All embraced and wept tears of joy.

The battle done, Pridon gave a proper burial to those of his men who had fallen in battle. Of the three hundred who left Pridon's land, only one hundred and sixty still lived. Then the knights and soldiers went through the town and slew every last foe. They gathered up all the treasure they could find, and in the end, they needed three thousand mules and camels to carry it all. Leaving sixty men to guard the looted city, they placed Nestan-Daredjan in a palanquin and rode for Gulansharo, where they intended to show their gratitude to the king and Patman, without whose aid Nestan would never have been found.

The Wedding of Tariel and Nestan-Daredjan

Tariel summoned a messenger and said, "Go to the king of the sea, who rules in Gulansharo. Invite him to meet us and be our guest. Tell him that we have sacked Kadjeti. That city is now his to rule, and the treasure it holds is his. Ask him also to bring Patman with him. We have rescued the one she holds dear, and we must put her fears to rest."

When the king of the sea learned of the deeds those brave knights had performed, he gladly assented to meet Tariel and his companions and agreed to have Patman accompany him. He rode out in train with Patman, his court, and his servants, and with mules laden with many precious gifts to give his hosts. The king was received with much joy by Pridon, Tariel, and Avtandil, and Patman and Nestan-Daredjan embraced and wept tears of joy.

"I never thought I would see you again. May God bless the ones who restored you to me," Patman said.

"And may God bless you, who is like a mother to me. When last you saw me, I was broken, but lo! Now I am whole, for the sun has been restored to my day," Nestan said.

The king of the sea's servants set up many bright pavilions, and the three friends exchanged costly gifts with him.

The king of the sea said to Tariel and Nestan, "There is no greater joy than to see two lovers united. It is my wish that you celebrate your wedding here with me, and there would be no greater honor to me than if you gave your assent."

So, it was that Tariel and Nestan-Daredjan plighted their troth, and the feasting, music, and dancing went on without stint for many days and nights.

Finally, it came time for the brave companions to depart. Again, they gave gifts to the king of the sea, and he presented them with many fine things. For Pridon and Avtandil there were the king's best horses, with tack and caparisons, and Tariel and Nestan were given jeweled crowns and bolts of the finest silk. The king also gave them a ship to take them home, and Tariel bowed humbly before the king in gratitude.

Soon it was time for farewells.

Tariel said to Patman, "I have not enough thanks to give to the one who is like a mother to my beloved Nestan. The best I can do is to give to you these jewels, pearls, and silks, which I hope you will take in recompense."

"O knight, my gratitude to you also knows no bounds. I am glad to have met you, and my heart rejoices for you and my dear Nestan, but I will be sad to see you go," Patman said.

Tariel said to the king of the sea, "Now we must depart for our lands. You will forever be as a father to us."

All of the friends embraced and shed bitter tears. Then the three brave companions and the lovely Nestan-Daredjan took ship and sailed for Pridon's land. They sent a messenger ahead to tell Asmat what had befallen and let Pridon's men know that their king was returning home unscathed. The companions rode in great joy to Pridon's castle, laughing and singing all the way, with Nestan-Daredjan carried in a beautiful palanquin so that she might make the journey unwearied.

The road to Pridon's castle was lined with cheering people. Asmat came running, and as soon as Nestan saw her, she jumped down from her palanquin and went to embrace her beloved sister.

"Never did I think to see you alive again. May God forever bless the ones who brought you back to me," Asmat said.

"I have heard how you tended my dear Tariel in the time of his grief and yours. How can I ever repay you?" Nestan said.

"It is payment enough to see my brother and sister in their happiness."

With those whose kinsmen had been killed in the battle, Tariel and Avtandil also wept.

"Their lives were given for my life, and that I'll not forget. May God look graciously upon them and bring them to rest with him in his kingdom forever," Tariel said.

Pridon caused another wedding feast to be held for Tariel and Nestan-Daredjan, and the whole palace made merry for eight full days.

At the end of the festivities, Tariel said to Pridon, "I ask a favor of you. Go to Avtandil and ask him what I might do for him since he has done so much for me."

Pridon went to Avtandil and gave him Tariel's message.

"There is nothing Tariel can do for me. I have wealth enough for any man, a liege lord who I am happy to serve, and when my beloved deems fit, her I shall wed. I wish only for Tariel's prosperity and happiness and to see him sit upon the throne of India," Avtandil replied.

Pridon reported Avtandil's reply to Tariel.

"I see. He is both proud and generous, but I'll not be thwarted. Tell him that I want to visit Rostevan, to ask forgiveness for having killed his men, and to ask Tinatin's hand for Avtandil," Tariel said.

Pridon again went to Avtandil and delivered Tariel's message. Avtandil's heart was wrung by Tariel's offer.

He went to Tariel himself and knelt before him. "Tariel, my dearest friend and brother, do not go to Rostevan. I've caused him enough grief, and I'll not be responsible for more. Nor shall I increase my beloved's woe since surely she blames me for Rostevan's unhappiness. If you remind them of that fateful day, their sorrow surely will increase."

"Never fear. I go to Rostevan as one king to another to pay my respects. That at least is courtesy, and I'll say what I need to say in the most diplomatic terms. May I ask for his daughter's hand to be given to one who is dearer to me than any brother? That is a request that one king may make of another, surely."

"To that, I will assent," Avtandil said.

The Wedding of Avtandil and Tinatin

The three brave companions left Pridon's realm and made for Tariel's cave, bearing Nestan-Daredjan and Asmat in a beautiful palanquin, accompanied by many of Pridon's soldiers. On the way, they hunted game, and when they got to the cave, the soldiers made their own camp nearby and cooked their meals, while inside the cave, Asmat roasted the meat for herself and her friends. The five friends had a merry meal together, and the place that once was the home of deep sorrow was now full of joy and laughter. When the meal was done, they explored the rest of the cave, and there they found even more treasure than they had thought possible to be collected in one place. Tariel and Nestan-Daredjan saw to it that all of Pridon's soldiers and generals were generously rewarded, and still, there was a great quantity of wealth remaining.

"My lord Pridon, I owe you a deep debt for your aid in finding my dear Nestan. I, therefore, would like to give all the rest of this treasure to you, to do with as you see fit," Tariel said.

"I don't know how to thank you for this. All I can say is that this treasure will be no substitute for your presence at my court. Your friendship and valor I prize above all the gold and jewels the world has to offer," Pridon said.

Pridon sent some of his men to fetch camels to carry the riches from the cave, and in the morning, the five companions rode to Rostevan's kingdom with the soldiers who had stayed behind. As they rode through the villages of Arabia, they noticed that all the people were in mourning.

"Who has died?" Pridon asked.

"They mourn for me. They think me dead because they don't know that I have returned from my quest," Avtandil replied.

When the friends and their retinue had made camp, Tariel wrote a letter to King Rostevan and summoned a messenger to take it to the palace. Tariel wrote:

> *To Rostevan, King of All Araby, from Tariel, King of India, greetings. My gracious King Rostevan, I write to you to as one king to another, on two accounts. On one fateful day many years ago, you sent out armed men to capture me, and I slew them. That was wrong of me, although equally was it wrong of you to assail me thus. But because of me, you suffered the loss of servants who were dear to you, and therefore, I beg your forgiveness. That is one part of my message to you. The other is to bring you good tidings, for with me travels a knight who knows no peer and for whom I know you have great affection. Avtandil is here, come at last to the place that is his home and that he holds so dear.*

When Rostevan read Tariel's letter, he shouted for joy. "Avtandil is home! No longer are we in mourning, for Avtandil has returned!"

Rostevan ordered his soldiers to saddle their mounts and go with him to greet Avtandil and conduct him and his friends to the palace with great pomp and rejoicing. He ordered drummers and musicians to come along and play cheerful, martial music all the way there and back. The soldiers all raced to do their king's bidding, for Avtandil was nearly as beloved to them as he was to Rostevan.

Tinatin, for her part, wept for joy that her dear Avtandil was returned to her.

Avtandil looked down the road toward the palace. He saw the great cloud of dust stirred up by Rostevan and his train and heard the faint sound of music and drums.

Avtandil went to Tariel and said, "I cannot meet Rostevan today. I am too ashamed of my disobedience. Let you and Pridon go and greet him first and see what his mood might be, and then send me news."

"Yes, that is proper. Never fear. We'll smooth the way for you," Tariel said.

Tariel and Pridon rode out to greet Rostevan, while Avtandil and Nestan-Daredjan stayed behind. Soon the kings met on the road. Seeing Tariel's beauty so smote Rostevan that he alit from his horse and bowed low to the younger man. Tariel likewise dismounted and bowed to Rostevan. The two kings embraced.

"My lord, will you sit with us in this meadow to converse?" Tariel asked.

Tariel and Rostevan seated themselves on the grass, and then Tariel said, "My lord Rostevan, I know that Avtandil is dearer to you than a son, but I must tell you that to me the world holds no one dearer than that brave knight, save my own Nestan-Daredjan. When I was on the brink of death, he saved me, and by his valor was my beloved returned to me. Avtandil has told me of his love for Tinatin. Therefore, I ask you on bended knee to grant your blessings to them and allow them to wed."

Then Tariel knelt before Rostevan and bowed low in supplication.

Rostevan was troubled by the way Tariel humbled himself.

Rostevan likewise knelt and bowed to Tariel, saying, "O valorous one, you needn't abase yourself for this request. No better son-in-law could I find than Avtandil, and my daughter has chosen him for her own. Tinatin is the wise ruler of this realm, and her judgment never falters."

Upon hearing Rostevan's reply, Pridon galloped back to the camp.

"Mount your horse! Come and meet Rostevan. He will grant all your desire," he told Avtandil.

Avtandil mounted and rode to the meadow with Pridon, his heart full of foreboding. He found Rostevan and Tariel standing there together, smiling. Avtandil dismounted, then threw himself on the ground and embraced Rostevan's feet.

"O my most gracious king, forgive me my disobedience. I did what I did only for love and not out of any wish to cause you sorrow."

Rostevan helped Avtandil to rise and embraced him. "Most valorous knight, dearer to me than any son, I am neither angered nor sorrowed by your deeds. I rejoice in them rather and would see you rejoicing, too, for today I give my blessing for you to wed our dearest Tinatin, who awaits you at the palace."

"I have no words to thank you. But before we ride to your palace, may we do one act of courtesy? Tariel's Nestan-Daredjan awaits us at our camp, and I wish that you would meet her and that she might accompany us on our return."

Rostevan gladly agreed, and when Nestan-Daredjan arose to greet him, he was smitten by her beauty and greeted her well as a king ought to do. Nestan mounted her palanquin and the knights their horses, and they all rode back to Rostevan's court with great rejoicing.

There they found Tinatin waiting, wearing her royal crown and bearing her scepter. Tariel and Nestan-Daredjan bowed before Tinatin, paid homage, and then led Tinatin to her throne. They took Avtandil by the hand and led him onto the dais to sit beside her.

Tinatin was overcome; she was pale and trembling.

Avtandil was robbed of speech and could do nothing but gaze at her.

Rostevan said, "My children, it is my heart's great delight to see you wed and rule wisely and well together when I am no more." Then he turned to his soldiers and vassals. "Here are your liege lords. Tinatin and Avtandil now rule this realm, and to them, you owe all fealty."

Tariel said to Tinatin, "How it gladdens my heart to see you united with he who is dearer than any brother. From this day forth, you shall be my sister, and I promise that always I will give you aid whenever you need it."

Rostevan commanded a great wedding banquet to be held for Tinatin and Avtandil. Every soldier received a gift, and Rostevan commanded that his treasury be opened and presents given to all the people according to their needs. To Pridon, Rostevan gave nine fiery steeds with saddles and tack, and to Tariel and Nestan, a great weight of gems and pearls.

The feasting and drinking went on without stint for many days. Such was the rejoicing that Tinatin and Avtandil, at last, were united.

All too soon, the celebrations came to an end.

Tariel went to Rostevan and said, "You have been the most exemplary host, and it gives me pain to have to leave your court. But my country has been overrun by enemies, and I must ride to save my kingdom."

"I weep to see you depart, but my armies are yours to command. Take my men and take back what is yours, and you and Nestan-Daredjan are forever welcome as my guests whenever you please to come," Rostevan said.

Pridon and Avtandil likewise pledged themselves to fight for Tariel, and soon they rode out at the head of Rostevan's army, whose numbers were swelled by the men Pridon had brought along.

Tinatin's parting with Nestan-Daredjan was bitter. They embraced and shed tears, pledging that they should be sisters forevermore.

Tariel, Pridon, and Avtandil took their leave of Rostevan, the valorous ones embracing the aged king with much affection. Tariel and Pridon pledged alliance with Rostevan, and Avtandil promised he would return as soon as Tariel had been restored to his throne.

The army wound its way from Arabia to India, and on the way, they met a group of Indian merchants whose heads were shorn and wore black, tattered clothing.

Tariel asked them, "Where are you from, and why are you dressed thus?"

"We are merchants from India. We wear mourning because our liege lord, Parsadan, is dead. What is worse is that Parsadan's daughter, whose loveliness rivals that of the sun, disappeared many years ago, and along with her Parsadan's most trusted knight. Seeing our realm in such disarray, the Khatavians attacked."

Hearing this, both Nestan-Daredjan cried out in grief. They wept and tore their hair at the news that Parsadan was dead.

"Woe to me!" Nestan cried.

"Alas, my father is dead! He who raised me as a son is no more! There is no light in my day!" Tariel cried.

"The queen yet lives, my lord and my lady," the merchants said, who now recognized Tariel and Nestan, "and our army still fights, but they are weary and outnumbered and besieged. We see that you have many men. Ride to the aid of our country! Overthrow King Ramaz and his men! Save our beloved queen!"

Tariel and his companions hastened to the field of battle. They saw the might of the Khatavian army but were not dismayed. Tariel sent some men to capture the Khatavian sentries, with orders that are brought back alive. Soon they were brought before Tariel, where they cast themselves at his feet and begged for mercy.

"I'll not slay you. Instead, I send you back to your king with a message. Tell Ramaz that Tariel is here, with the armies of Arabia, and with King Pridon and his men. Tell him that we'll gladly meet him on the field of battle but that he should prepare himself for defeat. Tariel is the rightful king of India and will spare no man in the slaughter to come. But if Ramaz is willing to surrender, he will be given safe-conduct, and we will use mercy toward him and his men," Tariel said.

Tariel sent the sentries back to Ramaz and then arrayed his army for battle. The standards of India, Arabia, and Mulghazanzar fluttered brightly in the wind. Seeing those three flags together made Ramaz's blood turn to water in his veins.

He went to Tariel and bowed low before him. "I surrender. Pride led me to invade when I saw that India was unprotected. I deserve to die for my presumption, I and all my viziers. But spare my soldiers. They are here because they were ordered to be and are innocent."

"I accept your surrender. You may go, and your soldiers will not be harmed. Do not raise a sword against us again, for next time, we will spare none of you," Tariel said.

Tariel rode to the fortress where the Indian army was besieged. At first, no one recognized him, but then he shouted, "It is I, Tariel, and I bring with me Nestan-Daredjan! We have returned!"

When the people realized who was outside the gate, they sent up a great cheer and sent out a party of soldiers to greet Tariel and his bride. Tariel and Nestan were reunited with the queen, and their tears of joy at their reunion were mixed with tears of sorrow for the passing of Parsadan. Avtandil and Pridon conveyed their condolences to the queen, who received those two knights with all the courtesy they deserved.

"Enough of your tears. Tariel and Nestan-Daredjan have returned to us. Let us have a feast to celebrate their union, and let them be set upon the throne of India," the queen said.

Tariel and Nestan were seated upon golden thrones, and at their side were Avtandil and Pridon.

Tariel summoned Asmat and said, "But for you, I would have perished. Any reward you ask for will be yours, and any man you wish to wed will be your husband."

"I wish nothing more than to continue to serve you and Nestan-Daredjan," Asmat said, and Tariel and Nestan received her service with much gratitude.

After many days of feasting and celebration, Avtandil went to Tariel and said, "My heart grieves to be parted from you, but my own Tinatin is waiting at home for me, and I would not have her sorrow. Alas, I must go."

Pridon said, "I must return to my land as well. Woe that I cannot stay. But I shall visit you as often as I may, and I beg you and Nestan-Daredjan often to be my guests at my own court."

Tariel gave Avtandil and Pridon many gifts, and Nestan gave Avtandil presents to give to Tinatin. The friends all embraced and wept as they said their farewells.

Pridon and his men rode with Avtandil and the Arabian army for a while, but then their paths parted, and each went to his own home.

So it was that Tariel was reunited with Nestan-Daredjan and that Avtandil wed Tinatin. These kings and queens ruled wisely and well and visited one another and their good friend King Pridon whenever possible. Their realms prospered under their care until the end of their lives.

Here's another book by Matt Clayton that you might like

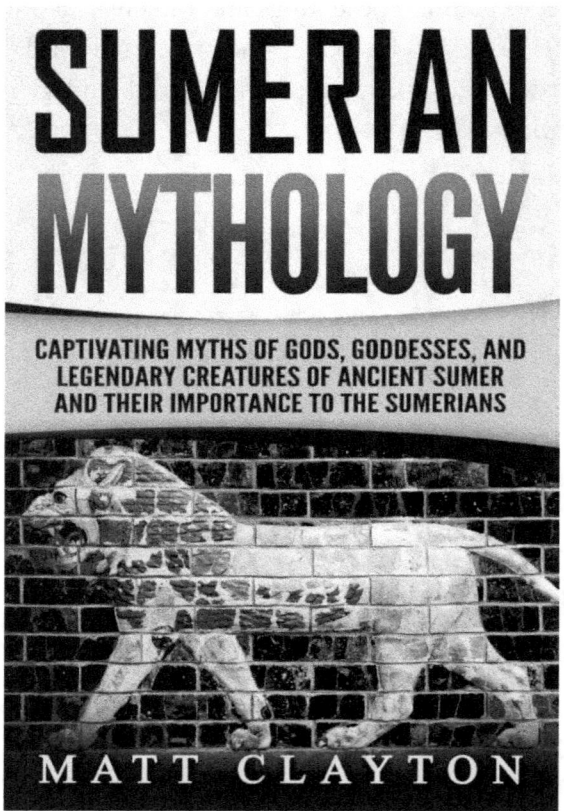

Free Bonus from Captivating History (Available for a Limited time)

Hi History Lovers!

Now you have a chance to join our exclusive history list so you can get your first history ebook for free as well as discounts and a potential to get more history books for free! Simply visit the link below to join.

Captivatinghistory.com/ebook

Also, make sure to follow us on Facebook, Twitter and Youtube by searching for Captivating History.

Bibliography

Arnot, Robert, and F.B. Collins, trans. *Armenian Literature.* New York: The Colonial Press, 1901.

Carpenter, Frances. *Wonder Tales of Horses and Heroes.* Garden City: Doubleday & Company, Inc., 1952.

Colarusso, John, trans. *Nart Sagas from the Caucasus: Myths and Legends from the Circassians, Abazas, Abkhaz, and Ubykhs.* Princeton: Princeton University Press, 2002.

Hedeghalh'e, Asker. *The Narts: Circassian Epos.* Vol. 1. Maikop: The Circassian Research and Science Institute, 1968). Excerpts translated by Amjad Jaimoukha, on the webpage *More Nart Tales.* <https://web.archive.org/web/20170113170919/http://www.reocities.com/Eureka/Enterprises/2493/nartsaga3.htm>. Accessed 21 January 2021.

Rustaveli, Shota. *The Knight in the Panther's Skin.* Translated by Lyn Coffin. Tbilisi: POEZIA Press, 2015.

Rust'haveli, Shot'ha. *The Man in the Panther's's Skin: A Romantic Epic.* Translated by Marjory Scott Wardrop. London: Royal Asiatic Society, 1912.

Seklemian, A. G. *The Golden Maiden and Other Folk Tales and Fairy Stories Told in Armenia.* Cleveland: The Helman-Taylor Company, 1898.

Shalian, Artin K., trans. *David of Sassoun: The Armenian Epic in Four Cycles.* Athens, OH: Ohio University Press, 1964.

Sideman, Belle Becker. *The World's Best Fairy Tales.* Pleasantville: The Reader's Digest Association, 1967.

Tolegian, Aram. "David of Sassoun: The Armenian Folk Epic." PhD diss., University of Southern California, 1960.

Toumanian, Hovhaness. "David of Sassoun." Translated by Thomas Samuelian. Arak29. Accessed 25 January, 2021. https://arak29.org/david-of-sassoon/

Tvirdíková, Michaela. *Folk Tales and Legends.* Translated by Vira Gissing. London: Cathay Books, 1981.

Anklesaria, Behramgore Temuras, trans. *Zand-Akasih: Iranian or Greater Bundahishn.* Bombay: n. p., 1956. Digital edition by Joseph H. Peterson, 2002. <http://www.avesta.org/mp/grb.htm> Accessed 16 December 2020.

Bleeck, Arthur Henry. *Avesta: The Religious Books of the Parsees.* 3 vols. Hertford: Stephen Austin, 1864.

Boyce, Mary, ed. and trans. *Textual Sources for the Study of Zoroastrianism.* Chicago: University of Chicago Press, 1984.

Citizen of Philadelphia, trans. *Bakhtiar Nameh, or The Royal Foundling: A Persian Story Exhibiting a Portraiture of Society in the East.* Philadelphia: Edward Parker, 1813.

Darmesteter, James, ed. and trans. *The Zend-Avesta.* 2nd ed. Oxford: Clarendon Press, 1895.

Eliade, Mircea. *Gods, Goddesses, and Myths of Creation: A Thematic Sourcebook of the History of Religion.* Part I: *From Primitives to Zen.* New York: Harper & Row, 1974.

Ferdowsi, Abolqasem. *Shahnameh: The Persian Book of Kings.* Dick Davis, trans. New York: Viking Penguin, 2006.

Keith, A. Barriedale, and Albert J. Carnoy. *Mythology of All Races.* Vol. 6: *Indian and Iranian.* Boston: Marshall Jones Company, 1917.

Ouseley, Sir William. *Bakhtyar Nameh, or Story of Prince Bakhtyar and the Ten Viziers.* London: Wilson & Co., 1801.

Rogers, Alexander, trans. *The Shah-namah of Fardusi.* 2 vols. London: Chapman & Hall, 1907.

Sykes, Ella C. *The Story-Book of the Shah, or Legends of Old Persia.* London: John MacQueen, 1901.

Warner, Arthur George, and Edmond Warner, trans. *The Shahnama of Firdausi.* 9 vols. London: K. Paul, Trench, Trübner & Co., Ltd., 1905.

West, Edward Wilson, trans. *Sacred Books of the East.* Vol. 5: *Pahlavi Texts*, Part I: *The Bundahis, Bahman Yast, and Shayast La-Shayast.* Oxford: Clarendon Press, 1880.

Wilson, Epiphanius. *Sacred Books of the East, Including Selections from the Vedic Hymns, the Zend-Avesta, the Dhammapada, the Upanishads, the Life of the Buddha, and the Koran.* London: The Colonial Press, 1902.